The Best *Stage Scenes* of 2007

The Best *Stage Scenes* of 2007

Edited by Lawrence Harbison
With a Foreword by D. L. Lepidus

SCENE STUDY SERIES

A SMITH AND KRAUS BOOK

Published by Smith and Kraus, Inc.
177 Lyme Road, Hanover, NH 03755
www.SmithKraus.com

First Edition: January 2008
10 9 8 7 6 5 4 3 2 1

Cover illustration: *Box Seat* by Lisa Goldfinger
Cover and text design by Julia Hill Gignoux,
Freedom Hill Design and Book Production

The Scene Study Series 1067-3253
ISBN 978-1-57525-588-0

Library of Congress Control Number: 2007939333

NOTE: These scenes are intended to be used for audition and class study; permission is not required to use the material for those purposes. However, if there is a paid performance of any of the scenes included in this book, please refer to the Rights and Permissions pages 199–202 to locate the source that can grant permission for public performance.

Contents

Scenes for One Man and One Woman

Scenes for Two Men

Scenes for Two Women

Foreword

In these pages you will find a rich and varied selection of scenes from recent plays, almost all of which have been published and are thus readily available to you when you have found that perfect scene to work on in class or to use for auditions. Many are for younger performers (teens through thirties) but there are also some excellent pieces for older performers. Many are comic (laughs), many are dramatic (generally, no laughs). Some are rather short, some are rather long. All represent the best in contemporary playwriting.

Many of the playwrights whose work appears here may be familiar to you — such as Ken Ludwig, Alan Ball, Melanie Marnich, Daisy Foote, A. R. Gurney, and Tom Dudzick, all of whom have had work produced in New York on or off Broadway; but you will also find some exciting new voices, up-and-comers like Anna Ziegler, Kathryn Walat, Rajiv Joseph, Jonathan Rand, Bert V. Royal, Boo Killebrew, and Trish Harnetiaux.

After seven years of doing these books for Smith and Kraus, I have decided to step aside and have turned over the reins to my old pal Lawrence Harbison, who knows as much about the theater and its plays and playwrights as anyone I know. It has been a very rewarding and very challenging task editing these anthologies; but now it is time to hang up my red pencil. I am retiring to Myrtle Beach, there to become one of those geezers who stands around all day in a kilt, sending foursomes of awful golfers off the first tee. In my free time I won't be reading plays: I'll be taking up bungee-jumping, hang-gliding, and alligator wrestling. There is life beyond the theater.

Break a leg.

D. L. Lepidus
Myrtle Beach, SC

Scenes for One Man and One Woman

All That I Will Ever Be
Alan Ball

Seriocomic
Cynthia & Omar — both probably thirties

Omar is a man of indeterminate nationality who as far as Cynthia knows works in an electronics store, where she has met him. Here, they are having a drink together.

(Omar and Cynthia are seated together at a table in some cheap but hip Los Angeles restaurant/bar, wearing the same clothes they wore in the previous scene. He's drinking a margarita, she's sipping a bourbon on the rocks. She gets tipsy pretty fast.)

CYNTHIA: I like that you drink Margaritas.

OMAR: Why?

CYNTHIA: It's cute.

OMAR: *(Doesn't like this.)* Cute? Why is it cute?

CYNTHIA: Well, most of the men I meet drink something a little more, you know, serious. Scotch, or a martini, or some wildly obscure imported beer. To prove what rugged individualists they all are.

OMAR: *(Shrugs.)* I like the way a Margarita tastes.

CYNTHIA: I used to drink Cosmos, but then I noticed like, every fucking D-girl in town drank Cosmos, it was like driving a Beamer three series, I mean, *such* a cliché. So now I drink bourbon.

(Omar makes a face, obviously not a fan of bourbon.)

CYNTHIA: *(Continued.)* So where are you from, Omar?

OMAR: Paris.

CYNTHIA: Seriously. I *love* Paris. Love it.

(Omar speaks in flawless French, much to Cynthia's delight.)

CYNTHIA: *(Continued.)* Have you been to the casino in Vegas?

OMAR: Yes.

CYNTHIA: Doesn't it like, encapsulate everything that's wrong with our culture? But it's still kind of fabulous in its own way? Like, it forces you to appreciate the unexpected baroqueness of modern life? You know what I mean? Like, the whole Meta aspect of like, all the faux experience that we can purchase so we don't have to have the actual experience?

(A beat.)

OMAR: I guess.

CYNTHIA: So where are you from originally?

OMAR: Paris.

CYNTHIA: Your parents are French? You look more ethnic than that.

OMAR: My grandfather was from Morocco.

CYNTHIA: Oh wow, my boss just went there with his lover. They said it was magnificent, except for the filth and the poverty and the time they got rocks thrown at them on the way back to their hotel. So what do you want to be?

OMAR: *(Not understanding.)* Excuse me?

CYNTHIA: You know, when you — I mean, you can't possibly want to spend the rest of your life working at Circuit Guys, right?

(Worried.)

Or do you?

OMAR: No, I definitely don't want to do that.

(Then.)

What do *you* want to be?

CYNTHIA: I want to be the first black woman in history to run a movie studio.

OMAR: Why?

CYNTHIA: Why not?

OMAR: Seriously, why?

CYNTHIA: Well, because I think that would be pretty goddamn cool. Not to mention extremely lucrative.

OMAR: But, why?

(Off her blank look.)

I mean, what are you doing for the world, for anyone?

CYNTHIA: Oh please. People need to be entertained.

OMAR: You think movies are entertaining? They're not. Especially American movies. That's bullshit. That's just distraction and mindless violence. Nobody *needs* that.

CYNTHIA: I disagree. Life is hard enough these days, I think people *crave* distraction —

OMAR: You think people *need* the thrill of seeing things blow up? Which wouldn't be a thrill at all if you'd grown up somewhere where you actually see that happen in real life, because you know what? In real life, it's not entertaining. Not one bit.

CYNTHIA: Well, no. I mean, nine eleven, duh. But. People have always enjoyed being frightened in controlled circumstances. Right? I mean, what about amusement park rides, or scary stories around the campfire? What about the hell mouths of the middle ages, or all of mythology, for that matter?

OMAR: *(Not listening.)* And it's always about white people. Julia Roberts and Brad Pitt and Cameron Diaz and Tom Cruise — they're so fucking vanilla, man, so fucking boring, and *they're* the ones we pick to live our lives for us?

CYNTHIA: Well, what about Will Smith —

OMAR: *(Ignoring her, overlapping.)* Only *we* didn't pick them.

CYNTHIA: — or Halle Berry, or Denzel —

OMAR: The truth is, the vast majority of the world has nothing in common with all these fucking pathetic white *nothings.*

CYNTHIA: But *you're* white. Right?

OMAR: Am I white? Are you kidding me?

CYNTHIA: Well, you're not black. Or Asian. Are you?

OMAR: Of course I'm white. But not to most white people.

CYNTHIA: *(Suddenly wary.)* Oh my God. Are you an actor?

OMAR: No.

CYNTHIA: Because if you are? Let's just end this right here, right now.

OMAR: I'm not an actor.

CYNTHIA: The last two guys I dated were actors, and one was like, pathologically incapable of thinking of anyone but himself. Ever. He just couldn't do it. Born without that gene. And the other one was gay.

OMAR: I said I'm not an actor, and I don't lie. But I am bisexual.

CYNTHIA: Well, as long as you're not an actor.

(Then.)

Are you really bisexual? Or are you just too scared to be totally gay?

OMAR: No, I really am.

CYNTHIA: I ate pussy once in college. Well, twice. The first time, I thought, wow, this is really interesting, I could really get into this, and then the second time, I wasn't on ecstasy, and it was like, ew.

(Stares at him, laughs.)

You *have* to be gay. Otherwise I wouldn't feel so comfortable talking to you like this.

OMAR: You're crazy. Eating pussy is one of the great joys of life. There is nothing else like it on earth.

CYNTHIA: Oh my God. You are so dramatic.

OMAR: I don't know which is a bigger pleasure, knowing you're making a woman feel beautiful, worshipped, and savored . . . or just losing yourself in the fact that you are right there up in the gate of fucking life, and you get to drink it up all you want, and she just wants you to go deeper, take longer, get her wetter and never, ever, fucking stop.

(A beat. Omar's cell phone goes off, with some sort of overly complicated ring. He turns it off without looking at it.)

CYNTHIA: Oh my God. Are you for real?

OMAR: You tell me.

END OF SCENE

All This Intimacy
Rajiv Joseph

Dramatic
Ty, mid to late twenties
Becca, late teens, early twenties

Ty teaches college level poetry and has recently published a well-received volume of poems. Becca, who is pretty and smart, has dropped by Ty's apartment to talk about poetry and, possibly, to go to bed with him.

(Ty opens his front door and Becca enters.)

BECCA: Hi!

TY: Hey there! What a surprise to get your call!

BECCA: I mean was in the neighborhood? I was having brunch. I totally love Brooklyn. It's so retro.

TY: Yeah, it is.
So . . . here you are.

BECCA: I hope I'm not intruding . . .

TY: No! I was just writing.

BECCA: Wow. Of course.
(She pulls out wine.)
I brought some wine.

TY: Wine!

BECCA: Because my new poem? It's about wine.

TY: Oh. that's good . . .good material . . .
Well, come on in. Make yourself at home . . .

BECCA: Awesome! This place is so cool! It's like a writer's lair.

TY: Yep. It is.

BECCA: So are you writing a new book of poetry?

TY: Uh, yes. that's what I'm trying to do . . .

BECCA: Is it going to be like *Labyrinth?*

TY: Well, I hope not *too* much like *Labyrinth.* I mean, I hope I'm growing as a poet.

BECCA: I can't believe you're going to *grow* as a poet.

TY: The things that concern you change. The things that inspire you change.

BECCA: What inspired you for *Labyrinth?*

TY: A woman.

BECCA: Oooh. A woman. Who?

TY: This was years ago, you know. Like four years ago.

BECCA: Yeah?

TY: I was in love with her. But she left me for another man who she then married.

BECCA: Oh, wow. I'm so sorry.

TY: Sometimes relationships end.

But you always have that distant hope they might begin again . . . but when someone gets married, then it's a whole different story. Marriage is so final.

BECCA: Yeah. I know. Except for, like, divorce.

TY: So I wrote about it. People like it.

BECCA: People love it.

TY: I don't know. Big picture is, nobody really reads poetry. I'll never sell large amounts of books.

BECCA: It doesn't matter how many you sell. If your poetry affects one person, then that's all that matters. That's how you change the world. You're changing the world with your poetry.

TY: *(To audience.)* Are you kidding me? You hear something like that out of a beautiful girl's mouth? What are you going to think? I'll tell you what you're *not* going to think: You're *not* going to think, *she's just a dumb lovestruck girl who's just flattering me.* You're thinking: *My poetry is changing the world.*

BECCA: *(To Ty.)* I mean, you're an artist. That's what you do.

TY: *(To audience.) I mean, I'm an artist. That's what I do.*

(Beat. Ty turns back to Becca.)

TY: *(To Becca.)* That's a little too much.

BECCA: No, I mean it.

TY: Well thank you. Thank you, Becca.

(Becca sees Maureen's kid's ball.)

BECCA: Oh, wow! What an awesome ball!

TY: That? Yeah, that's just a . . . it's a cool ball.

BECCA: Where did you get this?

TY: It's actually the kid next door's.

BECCA: Why do you have it?

TY: I play with him sometimes. You know, like babysit. I like kids.

BECCA: That's so sweet.

(She smiles at him. He smiles back.)

(She throws the ball at him. He catches it and tosses it back. She throws it back and they play catch, slowly closing the space between them.)

(Becca tosses the ball aside and kisses Ty. Ty starts kissing back. They start making out.)

TY: I'll go get a condom . . .

BECCA: I'm on the pill.

(Ty stares at her for a beat.)

TY: I'll go get a condom.

(Becca pulls him to her body.)

BECCA: It's okay. It's good.

(Ty goes with it.)

END OF SCENE

Asylum

Keith Aisner

Seriocomic
Gary, twenties
Angela, twenties

Due to a problem with sleeping, Gary has had trouble concentrating at work. He has been ordered by a suspicious boss to have a urine test, so he has come to the lab where Angela works.

(Drug testing center. Lights up on a desk with a computer resting on it and a chair in front of the desk. Sitting behind the desk is a frazzled Angela. She is entering data into the computer. Her door is open.)
(Enter Gary, standing in the doorway, holding his paperwork.)
(Angela notices him.)

ANGELA: Can I help you?

GARY: I think I'm supposed to be here.

ANGELA: Who told you that?

GARY: The, uh . . . lady at the front desk told me to come in here . . .

(Angela gets up and walks past Gary offstage.)

GARY: . . . after I finished filling out . . . the paperwork.

ANGELA: *(Offstage.)* Denise! No more, okay? I'm totally backed up here and I'm already an hour overdue for lunch. Okay?

(Angela returns and plunks down at her desk. Her hand is outstretched toward Gary. Gary approaches, then shakes it. Angela looks up, puzzled.)

ANGELA: Your paperwork please.

GARY: Oh. Yeah. Sorry.

(Angela takes his paperwork, glances at it for a moment.)

ANGELA: Have a seat, Gary. All right. I'm going to ask you some questions. Please answer them as honestly as you can.

GARY: Okey-doke.

ANGELA: Did you drive yourself here today?

GARY: Yes.

ANGELA: Do you drink alcohol?

GARY: Yes.

ANGELA: Would you say you drink alcohol rarely, occasionally, or frequently?

GARY: Occasionally.

ANGELA: Are you currently under the influence of alcohol or have you binged on alcohol within the last three days?

GARY: No.

ANGELA: Does your family have a history of alcoholism or drug abuse?

GARY: No.

ANGELA: After drinking do you experience lapses of memory or instances of lost time?

GARY: No.

ANGELA: Have you been or are you currently under the influence of any illegal drug or drugs, including, but not limited to PCP, marijuana or marijuana derivatives, methamphetamine . . . any opiates including opium, morphine, or heroin . . . cocaine or crack cocaine . . . mescaline, ecstasy, or psychedelic mushrooms?

GARY: What was that sixth one?

ANGELA: Uhhh, morphine?

GARY: Uh. No. Wait. Yeah, no. Uh . . . no.

ANGELA: Have you ever been convicted of a felony?

GARY: Tipped a cow once.

(Angela stares at him.)

GARY: But I was never caught. So no.

ANGELA: Okay, you know what? I hate this job. I hate everything about it. I hate that it invades people's privacy, I hate that it involves urine, and I hate that it involves me asking people humiliating and superfluous questions.

GARY: Whoa, wait, I . . . I apologize, I didn't mean to . . .

ANGELA: No. No . . . I'm sorry . . .

GARY: No, I shouldn't have . . .

ANGELA: No . . . it's . . . just this job. You didn't do anything wrong.

GARY: I was being a smartass.

ANGELA: It's just . . . I've only been here for a few months and . . . I don't think . . . I don't know.

GARY: *(Beat.)* I noticed you used the word "superfluous."

ANGELA: Yeah?

GARY: Right on. That's great.

(Angela laughs.)

GARY: No, seriously, I think that's fantastic.

ANGELA: People say "superfluous" all the time.

GARY: No, they don't. Really. I mean, they should . . . "superfluous" is a fine word . . . but most of the folks who could get past the "super" part usually end up adding "-bowl" or "-size it." It's very depressing.

ANGELA: *(Laughs again.)* So why are you here? You don't have to answer that.

GARY: They don't tell you.

ANGELA: No. I just ask the questions and get a sample.

GARY: My job. I've been kinda low energy lately and my boss thinks I must be high or hung over, but I'm not. I'm just tired.

ANGELA: Well, get some sleep.

GARY: Thank you, I'll do that.

ANGELA: Okay. Moving on . . . are you currently on probation?

GARY: No.

ANGELA: And are you currently using any prescription medication?

GARY: No.

ANGELA: Okay. Good. I'm running a little behind so I've still gotta get your kit set up. I'll be right back.

(Exit Angela.)

(Beat.)

(Re-enter Angela.)

ANGELA: I'm sorry, I forgot to ask you. Do you have enough for a sample? Or do you need me to get you some water or coffee?

GARY: *(Offering a thumbs-up:)* Bladders-ho!

ANGELA: Great.

(Angela starts to leave.)

GARY: Hey!

ANGELA: What?

GARY: What's your name? I mean, if it's okay to ask.

ANGELA: *(Smiling.)* It's okay. It's Angela.

GARY: Hello Angela.

ANGELA: Hi.

(Angela exits.)

(Gary stretches out in the chair. After a few moments his head begins to

droop and the lights dim to total darkness. A hard-driving rock tune such as Love and Rockets' "Motorcycle" quickly fades in to loud. By the time Gary's head drops lowest, ultraviolet lights brighten and . . .)

(Enter Dancer . . .)

(. . . from out of nowhere. The patterns of glow that appear on her give an abstract appearance of a cheerleader. As the music starts to heighten she begins to dance seductively. She teases the spaces around his body. Then the music crescendos and she lands her hand upon his shoulder. Simultaneously, Gary awakes, the lights switch back to normal, the music cuts out, and Angela is revealed as having been Dancer.)

ANGELA: Hey, wake up.

GARY: Huh?

ANGELA: I didn't mean for you to sleep here.

GARY: No I was just resting.

ANGELA: You were not, you were sleeping. You jerked awake when I touched you.

GARY: No, you just startled me. Honest.

ANGELA: Okay.

GARY: Do you dance?

ANGELA: You mean professionally?

GARY: Yeah.

ANGELA: Are you asking me out?

GARY: No!

ANGELA: You're certain?

GARY: Absolutely.

ANGELA: *(Beat.)* No, I've never danced professionally.

GARY: Okay.

(Angela produces the sealed piss cup and hands it to Gary.)

ANGELA: Bathroom's right behind you.

(Gary rises, takes it, and exits.)

(Gary re-enters.)

GARY: Okay, now I'm asking you out.

ANGELA: Why don't you pee in the cup first?

END OF SCENE

BFF

Anna Ziegler

Dramatic
Lauren, twenties
Seth, twenties

Here Lauren attempts to tell Seth the truth for the first time in the play. She has not only been hiding her real name from him but more importantly who she really is. Seth has been an open and generous boyfriend. Though he is still kind to her, he doesn't want to resume their relationship.

(Lauren stands at Seth's front door, knocking. The whole scene has a kind of fast and frantic quality; Lauren, even when she has Seth's attention, seems to be trying urgently to get it, to say something.)

LAUREN: Um, Seth. It's . . . me *(Beat.)* I know you're home because . . . well, I saw you walk home. You had a bag from Changs and I can smell your food, Peking Duck or something, so I know you're in there . . . and I feel like . . . I mean, I really need to see you. I mean, Seth, I really need to see you . . . I need to —

(Seth opens the door.)

You opened the door.

So, hi. *(Beat.)*

How are you?

SETH: I'm not going to talk to you.

LAUREN: But you opened the door.

(He begins to close the door.)

No! Seth.

(He opens the door a little.)

SETH: I'm not going to talk to —

LAUREN: I have to tell you something! I have to; I have to.

SETH: *(Opening the door, and angrily:)* Like what, that you're insane?

LAUREN: No, Seth. I mean, yes, I mean in a way. Yes —

SETH: Try making some sense. A coherent thought would be nice.

LAUREN: Don't get mad, please —

SETH: Don't get mad? Look, if you're crazy just tell me right now that you're crazy — because I mean, I thought . . . even though you were a little . . . mysterious . . . I thought I knew you. And it's not like I don't have my own problems, I mean — do I need this? Do I need someone so . . . messed up? How messed up are you exactly?

LAUREN: Eliza died.

SETH: Great.

LAUREN: No, I mean. She was my best friend. And she died. When we were fourteen.

SETH: Yup.

LAUREN: I'm not lying.

SETH: No, of course not.

LAUREN: Please, Seth.

SETH: Please, what?

LAUREN: I was just a kid.

SETH: Uh-huh.

LAUREN: And I made an awful mistake and ever since then, I've been, well, inside of it. It just goes on and on. Like I'm outside of time and I can't get back in.

SETH: You're outside of time.

LAUREN: *(Looking down and quietly.)* And the problem is, there aren't punishments!

SETH: What are you talking about?

LAUREN: For little girls who do bad things. Who are mean and selfish and trying to grow up. There are no punishments. No one blamed me even though it was my fault, Eliza dying. I just went back to school and sat at my desk and ate my lunch and did my algebra homework. I just, I mean, did my homework like anyone else.

SETH: What do you mean it was your fault?

LAUREN: I abandoned her.

SETH: Like in a sinking ship, on a desert island? What are you trying to tell me?

LAUREN: I made other friends and I left her behind.

SETH: Uh-huh.

LAUREN: It was when she needed me most.

SETH: And?

LAUREN: And then she got very thin and sort of faded away.

(Beat.)

SETH: And you think that was your fault?

LAUREN: I know it was.

SETH: When I was fourteen, my best friend was Mark Hickman. When I was fourteen and two weeks, Mark Hickman wouldn't look me in the eye, literally ran away from me down crowded hallways. I didn't kill myself.

LAUREN: No, for so long after she died, I didn't get out of bed. My parents thought I might never recover and they were right, in a way, even though I did eventually get out of bed and sort of go through the motions. That is, until I met you, when I thought, and I know this is crazy, I thought for the first time, wow, Eliza would have really liked this guy; she would have really liked him, the way he's unpretentious and open and caring and brave. That's the kind of man she would have liked. And so . . . I don't know . . . I just said her name. Because she was with me anyway. Because it just came out that way —

SETH: God.

LAUREN: And I was okay for a while because everything was new, because it hadn't gotten serious.

SETH: Uh-huh.

LAUREN: But then things got confusing because I still couldn't give her up, even when I wanted to —

SETH: Liza —

LAUREN: Seth, my name's Lauren.

(Beat.)

SETH: Lauren.

LAUREN: Lauren.

(Beat.)

And I can show you where I grew up and I can meet your friends and you can meet my parents, even though they'd be shocked that you really exist, that anyone exists who could have helped me . . . emerge. And you can call me at work even though I kind of keep to myself there and people would talk if I got a call. I mostly spend my time underwater, in the tanks, running tests. But now I don't want to. I don't want to anymore. I don't want to anymore.

SETH: Lauren.

LAUREN: I don't know. Maybe we can at least be friends? If . . .

SETH: I don't want to be your friend.

LAUREN: Okay.

SETH: It's just that . . . and this is me talking and not my therapist or Trevor or anyone. It's just that, I can't keep putting myself through, well this, or you, I mean. I can't keep putting myself through you.

LAUREN: I know.

SETH: If I could, I would.

LAUREN: I understand that.

SETH: I'm sorry.

LAUREN: I'm sorry too.

(Long beat.)

SETH: But what do you think.

LAUREN: What do you mean?

SETH: True or false.

LAUREN: What?

SETH: It's possible.

LAUREN: What is?

SETH: Happiness.

LAUREN: Oh. I don't know.

SETH: But take a stab at it.

(Beat.)

LAUREN: Okay, I think it's possible.

SETH: You do?

LAUREN: Yes.

SETH: Why?

LAUREN: Well otherwise, how would we get through each day?

END OF SCENE

Bhutan

Daisy Foote

Dramatic
Frances, late teens
Warren, twenties

Frances and Warren are brother and sister, who live with their mother. Both have dreams. Warren is in love and Frances hopes some day to be able to go to college.

(Frances comes into the kitchen. Warren is there cleaning up after his mother and aunt from the night before.)

FRANCES: Look it's the birthday boy . . .

WARREN: Where's Mary?

(Warren pours them both coffee.)

WARREN: *(Continued.)* Her car's not in the driveway.

FRANCES: She's probably driving Aunt home.

WARREN: Aunt stayed here last night?

(Frances nods.)

WARREN: *(Continued.)* They been down to the Molly?

(Frances doesn't respond.)

WARREN: *(Continued.)* What kid of shape were they in?

FRANCES: What kind of shape do you think they were in?

WARREN: Check the attitude, Lady.

FRANCES: I'm sorry, I'm just really tired. Aunt kept kicking me all night. Did you have a good time?

(He grins.)

WARREN: Anna's sister and brother in law, they were wicked nice. Told me and Anna to come and stay whenever we want. Their house is our house.

(A beat.)

You are not going to believe what I did this morning.

FRANCES: What?

WARREN: I went to church.

FRANCES: You did not.

WARREN: Anna's sister and brother in law always go. Anna wanted to go, and I didn't want to seem like an asshole. And you know it wasn't so bad. I barely heard what the sermon was. The guy was going on about some story in the Bible and how to apply it to your life. Whatever. But being there with Anna and her family, it was nice . . . it was . . . orderly.

(He drinks his coffee.)

WARREN: *(Continued.)* So what do you think, you think Anna would make a decent sister in law?

FRANCES: Are you serious?

WARREN: We talked about it last night.

FRANCES: Doesn't she want to go to college?

WARREN: It's not written in stone. Anna's a pretty old fashioned girl. And I think it's always bugged her that her Ma worked full time when she didn't have to. Anna wants to be there for our kids.

FRANCES: You've already talked about kids?

WARREN: We talk about everything.

(Frances gets cereal out of the cupboard.)

FRANCES: You want some cereal?

WARREN: No thanks.

(She pours the cereal, gets milk and so on.)

WARREN: *(Continued.)* Course, Anna's parents are going to go postal when they find out. Especially her Ma, always talking about Anna being a big time lawyer some day. But she doesn't know Anna like I do.

(Frances sits at the table and starts to eat her food.)

(Warren grabs a piece of paper and a pencil. He starts to make a list.)

WARREN: *(Continued.)* That window in your room still broken?

FRANCES: Yes. And the light in the bathroom is still making that popping sound.

(A beat.)

When are you going to tell Mary?

WARREN: I'll tell her.

FRANCES: When?

WARREN: *(Snapping.)* When I goddamn feel like it.

(Frances backs off.)

WARREN: *(Continued.)* I'll tell her, Frances. Soon. I promise. Anna and I need to talk through a few things first, get our plans good and set before we tell Mary or Anna's parents. We want them to see how serious we really are . . . that they can't change our minds.

(A beat.)

Anna says she wants you to call her this week. Something about meeting her at the Big Sip . . . she's crazy for that place . . . always drinking some ice mint mocha crap.

FRANCES: Why does she want to meet me?

WARREN: Because she's going to be your sister-in-law.

(He indicates the coffee pot.)

WARREN: *(Continued.)* This is the last of it, you want anymore?

FRANCES: You take it.

(He pours.)

FRANCES: *(Continued.)* Warren, did you ever think about college?

WARREN: No reason to. Always knew I'd be a plumber, don't need college for that.

FRANCES: Mrs. Letemkin was talking about Columbia in New York where she taught . . . she thought I might like it.

WARREN: You'd want to live there?

FRANCES: I don't know.

WARREN: Last place I'd ever want to live. A hell of a lot of money . . . college . . . money we don't have. So if you're at all serious, you better start thinking now about how you'll pay for it.

(The furnace bangs.)

WARREN: *(Continued.)* Did you hear that?

FRANCES: The furnace. It woke me up last night it was so loud.

WARREN: I'll try and fix it later. Need to keep it going until I've got the money to help Mary pay for a new one. If it ever stopped working and I wasn't here, the wood stove will keep the downstairs warm . . . but the upstairs . . . I'll teach you how to drain the pipes so they won't freeze and burst.

(A beat.)

You still want me to build you those shelves?

FRANCES: If you have time.

WARREN: I'll find it.

(He is scribbling on his list again.)

FRANCES: You remember that country I was telling you about . . . the one Mrs. Letemkin visited before she moved here . . . Bhutan? Did you know about it, Warren? The country. Did you even know it was there?

WARREN: No.

FRANCES: Don't you think that's weird?

WARREN: No.

FRANCES: A whole country and we didn't even know it was there. And if Mrs. Letemkin had never moved here, we still wouldn't know about it. A whole country filled with people and rivers and lakes and cities. With houses and families. And we never would have known it was there. That bothers me, Warren. It really does.

WARREN: Well, stop thinking about it.

FRANCES: I can't do that. I keep trying to imagine myself there and every time . . . I come back here . . . to this kitchen. And I'm here with you and Mary. I try to put myself on one of those mountains Mrs. Letemkin climbed or in one of those temples she visited, but this kitchen is all I see.

WARREN: You, me and Mary . . . ?

FRANCES: Uh huh.

WARREN: Well, look again, Lady, because I'm not there. I'm with Anna in my house on ten acres with a view of the mountains. That other picture. . . get it out of your mind. Just toss it out.

FRANCES: I can't.

WARREN: Get it out . . . out . . .

(He starts to tickle her.)

FRANCES: Stop it.

(He tickles her more, she's laughing.)

WARREN: Is it out yet?

(And laughing . . .)

WARREN: *(Continued.)* Is it out yet?

FRANCES: *(Screaming.)* Yes . . . yes . . .

WARREN: No more pictures . . . say it . . . no more pictures . . .

FRANCES: *(Shrieking.)* No more pictures . . . NO MORE PICTURES!

(She breaks loose and runs, Warren chasing her and grabbing her again, tickling her some more. She is screaming with laughter . . .)

END OF SCENE

Blur

Melanie Marnich

Dramatic
Joey and Dot. Both seventeen.

Dot has just been introduced to Joey by her friend Francis, while they are hanging out at a pier. And the world transforms.

JOEY: That was Francis.
DOT: I know.
JOEY: She's really nice. But she tries hard not to be. Because of her face.
DOT: It's not that bad.
JOEY: Tell her that.
DOT: She your girlfriend?
JOEY: No! No. I mean, no. She's not. N. O. No.
(Awkward silence. Dot cleans her glasses on her shirt.)
JOEY: Can I tell you a secret?
(Dot nods.)
JOEY: I usually throw the fish back, too. Except the ones I eat.
DOT: I felt so stupid.
JOEY: You did a nice thing. Because you're, like, a nice person.
DOT: Thanks.
(Geeky silence.)
JOEY: I'm sorry about your eyes.
DOT: Pfft. *(As in "they're not that bad.")*
(More geeky silence.)
JOEY: Um. Um. Um. Um.
DOT: Is there something you want to ask me?
JOEY: Um. *(He slaps a bug on his neck.)* I uh, I work at the zoo.
DOT: Really?
JOEY: I'm, you know, in charge.
DOT: Of the zoo?

JOEY: Sort of. Well. In charge of cleaning. The cages. The lemurs are in heat right now so things have been a little crazy. But when things, like, settle down, maybe, I dunno, maybe you could visit and I'll buy you a cotton candy.

(Dot takes off her glasses.)

JOEY: Should you do that?

DOT: Why not?

JOEY: Won't you tip over or something?

DOT: Bad eyes. Not bad balance.

JOEY: Can you see me?

DOT: Hm. Closer.

(He takes a step.)

DOT: Closer.

(Another step.)

DOT: Closer.

(Another.)

DOT: Closer.

(Another.)

DOT: Closer.

(He's really close.)

JOEY: Can't you see me yet?

DOT: I could see you a few steps ago, genius.

(They kiss.)

END OF SCENE

Blur

Melanie Marnich

Dramatic
Dot and Joey, early twenties

Dot and Joey have moved into an apartment together and Dot left home. Dot has just spent the day at the Center for the Blind, where she is being taught how to read Braille by a blind man who embodies her fears, her future and her potential power.

(Dot and Joey in apartment, that night. Joey repairs one of his work boots with duct tape.)

DOT: Joey?

JOEY: Yeah.

DOT: Something happened today.

JOEY: Nooo kidding. Lynch got promoted. To what, I don't know. *(He rips tape loudly.)* Torkelson got a raise. For what, don't know. *(Rips tape loudly.)* Gerber quit to work for the aquarium. For who, I don't —

DOT: Joey?

JOEY: What. *(Rips tape.)*

DOT: I went to the Braille place today.

JOEY: Hm.

DOT: To practice.

JOEY: Good.

DOT: There was this guy. He talked to me.

JOEY: Blind guy?

DOT: Yeah. He didn't really *talk.* He sort of . . . flirted.

JOEY: Takes some nerve.

DOT: Not just flirted. More like *hounded.* Flirted and hounded. *(Silence.)*

DOT: Not in a bad way. Not a good way, either, but . . .

JOEY: *(Starting to lose patience — and security.)* In what way, then?

DOT: I don't know.

JOEY: You got rid of him, though, right?

DOT: I think he thought he was helping.

(Joey loudly rips tape.)

DOT: He kept talking to me. Like I'm blind. And I kept saying I'm not, but he kept going on and on. He talked about what the blind see. In dreams. Dreams of blood, explosions, violence. Or dreams full of movement, of travel around the world.

JOEY: So you didn't get rid of him.

DOT: He says he flies, around and around. Because the blind can't do it in real life, they dream it. And then he said —

JOEY: You're trying to say you *like* this guy?

DOT: No! No, I just — He scared me a little, but —

JOEY: So what do you want me to do, huh? Want me to go punch this asshole in the nose for you?

DOT: He's not an asshole.

JOEY: So you *do* like him.

DOT: No. Listen.

JOEY: Maybe you want me to go pick a fight with some handicapped bastard because he rattled your cage a little?

DOT: I'm trying to tell you the whole story.

JOEY: 'Cause I won't do it. I'm not gonna be your dumb thug.

DOT: Joey!

JOEY: What? You think everybody has to be nice to you because you can't see so good?

DOT: I was just telling you what happened —

JOEY: Fight your own battles. I'm busy. Got my own problems. You don't have to have some freak disease to have problems, you know.

DOT: Freak disease?!

JOEY: No one allowed to have a bad day around you? Always have to be in a good mood for you?

DOT: No!

JOEY: You had a bad day. So fuckin' what. Go duke it out with the guy because I'm not gonna.

DOT: But I don't want you to. Oh. Oh. I get it now. You're scared, aren't you? You, Mister Big Tough Alpha Male.

JOEY: Back off.

DOT: Gotta show 'em who's boss. Gotta mark your territory.

JOEY: Shut up.

DOT: And you're scared of this guy.

JOEY: Shut up.

DOT: You're scared and you're jealous.

JOEY: Right.

DOT: You're a chicken.

JOEY: You surprised? You didn't guess that I was a big fat chicken shit?! You didn't figure that out? I know you can't see, but —

DOT: Fuck you.

JOEY: Coward? Loser? Go on. Say it. Say "Fuck You, You Piece Of Shit."

(She doesn't.)

JOEY: I got problems too, you know. You're not the only one. I have pressures. You think it's easy staying at the bottom of the ladder?

DOT: What kind of pressure is that?

JOEY: You think I like spending every day knee-deep in shit?!

DOT: God, you are a loser!

JOEY: Good. Now say "I am changing." Say, "I am changing and you're not." Say, "I am changing and there's this other guy who understands." Go ahead, say it. *(He keeps trying to grab her, she keeps wrenching out of his grasp.)* Say it! Say it!

DOT: Stop — Stop it! You're hurting me!

(He stops.)

JOEY: I'm a different animal from you, Dot. You come home and tell me about this guy who knows things, who can teach you things. Who's more like you than I'll ever be. Who am I? Maybe — Maybe I'm more scared than you.

DOT: I just wanted to tell you about the dreams. The dreams he described. Because I have some of them already. The bloody ones. The beautiful ones. The travel-around-the-world ones. He was right about everything.

END OF SCENE

Bye, Bye, Margarita
Gavin Lawrence

Dramatic
Margarita, mid to late twenties
Richard, forties

Margarita, who happens to be addicted to certain types of men, has come to tour the university and hopes to start a relationship with Richard, who is in charge of the Russian Studies program. He is also trying to move on with his married life after having a student and ex-lover commit suicide after their break-up.
Please Note: This scene takes place in a café and is abridged. A brief appearance by the waiter, Dante, has been cut.

(Margarita enters. She approaches the table.)
MARGARITA: Professor Pearson?
RICHARD: Richard. Margarita?
MARGARITA: Hi. I thought you'd be older.
RICHARD: Sorry to disappoint you.
MARGARITA: No, it's okay. I mean, it's fine — you're fine.
RICHARD: Please sit down.
(Margarita sits.)
MARGARITA: Thanks.
RICHARD: So, how was your flight?
MARGARITA: Bumpy. But it was worth it.
RICHARD: Worth it?
MARGARITA: I've been accepted to four different graduate programs. I wanted to be sure before I made my decision.
RICHARD: Well, I have three other candidates on hold, so let's eat and get you up to campus.
MARGARITA: No need.
RICHARD: What do you mean?

MARGARITA: I've made up my mind. That's why it was worth it. I want to go to your school.

RICHARD: You haven't seen the school.

MARGARITA: Look, I've been to other schools. You're the only adviser who agreed to meet me . . . outside of the school. You know, off-campus.

RICHARD: And that's why you want to go to the U?

MARGARITA: I read about you. I know what you've been through.

RICHARD: What's that?

MARGARITA: Did you love her?

RICHARD: What do you mean?

MARGARITA: The student who committed suicide — did you love her?

RICHARD: What right do you have? What do you want?

MARGARITA: I sent you a picture, and you like pretty grad students.

RICHARD: That's all in the past.

MARGARITA: I'm flirting.

RICHARD: I'm married, Margarita.

MARGARITA: I know. And you're sad. Here, this is for you.

(She takes a book from her bag and gives it to him.)

RICHARD: Mikhail Bulgakov. "The Master and Margarita." I teach Russian Literature. I already own this book.

MARGARITA: What's your wife's name?

RICHARD: My wife?

MARGARITA: What's her name?

RICHARD: Frieda.

MARGARITA: Really? Mine's Margarita.

RICHARD: I know. Look, I don't know if I gave you the wrong idea . . .

MARGARITA: I love that book. I feel like it was written for me. My father named me after this Margarita. I love Bulgakov. I love Russian Literature.

RICHARD: Why?

MARGARITA: It's not cluttered with sentimentality.

RICHARD: I know a few writers who might disagree with you.

MARGARITA: Personally?

RICHARD: No.

MARGARITA: Who?

RICHARD: Turgenev, Pushkin, Lermontov.

MARGARITA: They never met me. Ready to go?

(She gets up. He gets up.)

RICHARD: Where are we going?

MARGARITA: I suddenly have a strong desire to see your office.

RICHARD: I don't think that's a good idea.

MARGARITA: Scared?

RICHARD: Married — very married . . .and maybe a little scared.

MARGARITA: Why?

RICHARD: What's really going on here, Margarita? Who are you?

END OF SCENE

Check Please, Take 2
Jonathan Rand

Comic
Jackie & Guy, both probably late twenties

Guy & Jackie are on a blind date. Guy has recently broken up with another woman.

(Acronyms in this scene are displayed in all caps for ease of understanding. They should not necessarily be yelled or emphasized.)

GUY: Hi!

JACKIE: Hi!

GUY: Nice to meet you.

JACKIE: Same here!

GUY: So right off the bat, I have to be honest with you — this is the first time I've ever gone out with someone I met online.

JACKIE: Really? Oh, I do it all the time.

GUY: Yeah?

JACKIE: Sure. It's the only way to date, IMHO.

(Beat.)

GUY: I'm sorry?

JACKIE: IMO, it's the only way to date.

GUY: IMO?

JACKIE: Ahhhh, I didn't realize! So if you're a noob, then you don't understand online lingo!! LOL!

GUY: Right, so I don't —

JACKIE: That is so cute! LOL, ROFLMAO!

GUY: I'm —

JACKIE: OMG, you must be so lost right now, OMFG!

GUY: I really don't follow you.

JACKIE: Anyway, anyway — gimme the 411 about yourself, shyguy626! What do you do in your free time?

GUY: Well, ah . . . actually, I just started windsurfing lessons.

JACKIE: R0X0R! *(If this expression is too obscure, feel free to use "Kewl!" instead.)*

GUY: I you don't mind me being honest, I've had a lot more free time for starting new hobbies after my ex-girlfriend and I broke up.

JACKIE: Uhhh, TMI!

GUY: What?

JACKIE: JK! JK! JK!

GUY: What's "TMI"?

JACKIE: TMI! *(She lays it out for him in plain English:)* "T" . . . Okay? Then "M." And you finish it off with "I." TMI.

(Guy decides to leave that confusing response behind.)

GUY: So — what about you? What do you like to do?

JACKIE: Oh, gosh . . . So many things. Well, I'd say I spend about half of my workday on MySpace, and the rest split between Facebook, LiveJournal, and Friendster. *(If any websites in this scene are out of date, please replace with current equivalent.)* And when I'm lookin' for luuuuv — JK, LOL — I spend my time on, you know, the usual places: Match.com, E-Harmony, J-Date.

GUY: J-Date?

JACKIE: Yep!

GUY: Isn't that where Jewish singles meet other Jewish singles?

JACKIE: Yep!

GUY: Didn't your profile say you were Catholic?

JACKIE: Yep!

GUY: Then why are you on J-Date?

JACKIE: Why are *you* on J-Date?

GUY: I'm *not* on J-Date.

JACKIE: Well, agree to disagree.

GUY: What?

JACKIE: Okay, so I have a few more FAQs for you, shyguy626. E.G.: Where do you see yourself in five years?

GUY: I'm sorry, I have to ask: Why are you calling me shyguy626?

JACKIE: It's your SN. Why wouldn't I call you shyguy626?

GUY: My — Ohh, my screen name. I don't know . . . You wouldn't want me to call you — uh . . .

JACKIE: CutiePatootie5!

GUY: Right, CutiePatootie5.

JACKIE: OMG, yes I would!

GUY: All right . . .

JACKIE: BTW, it is soooo adorable that you don't understand what I'm saying. You are TCFW. It's like I speak English and you speak Canadian.

GUY: Th —

JACKIE: I like it. You make me laugh. Winky face.

GUY: W —

JACKIE: OMG, you must be so confused; you're like G2G, TTYL.

GUY: Okay, stop for a second. I've gotta ask — because I've honestly never heard anyone use screen names . . . or those internet abbreviations . . . out loud: Is it normal for a person to do that?

(Pause. She is blindsided.)

GUY: What?

JACKIE: Frowny face.

GUY: Oh, I didn't mean to offend you —

JACKIE: Frowny face with tears.

GUY: Look, could we just —

JACKIE: WTF.

GUY: I'm sorry? I don't under —

JACKIE: W . . . T . . . F-ing . . . F!

GUY: I honestly have no idea what that means.

(Jackie turns away, offended.)

GUY: What? What's wrong?

JACKIE: NOYB.

GUY: Can we talk about what's wrong?

JACKIE: No. EOD.

GUY: I wish I knew what you were saying.

JACKIE: You know what? You are being so inappropriate? — I'm going to file a complaint to the website where we met, and then do everything in my power to get you blacklisted from online dating.

GUY: What? That's not fair!

JACKIE: And that will prevent you from dating anyone like me EVER AGAIN!

(She runs off.)

(Pause.)

(He says matter-of-factly, without sarcasm:)

GUY: That's upsetting. Sarcastic winky face.

(Blackout.)

END OF SCENE

Check Please, Take 2
Jonathan Rand

Comic
Paul & Girl

Paul & Girl are on a blind date. She is coming off a recent breakup.

GIRL: Hi!
PAUL: Hi!
GIRL: So . . . tell me about yourself.
PAUL: Well, I work in hedge funds —
GIRL: Cool! That's where you buy stocks at a low value and then sell it to banks? Wait, no. I have that completely wrong.
PAUL: Don't worry about it.
GIRL: Sorry. I actually do know more about the market, it's just that — honestly — I'm nervous. I'm so terrible at these things.
PAUL: What — dates?
GIRL: Yeah.
PAUL: Ahh, don't worry about it. I try not to be too judgmental on dates. They're set up to be so high-pressure.
GIRL: True.
PAUL: And it's a wasteland out there, so maybe it's easier to handle because I'm less optimistic than I used to be.
GIRL: That's so refreshing to hear. I thought it was just me.
PAUL: No, it's pretty awful.
GIRL: But you don't seem the least bit flustered. How do you stay so calm?
PAUL: It helps to have a lot of first-hand experience with relationships.
GIRL: You've done a lot of dating?
PAUL: Yeah. Dating, marriage, blah blah blah.
GIRL: You're divorced?
PAUL: No, no.
GIRL: It's totally okay if you are. I dated a guy once who had multiple ex-wives.
PAUL: Oh, don't worry about that. I don't have any ex-wives —

GIRL: Okay.

PAUL: — I have wives.

(Pause.)

GIRL: I'm sorry, I thought I heard you say—

PAUL: I have wives.

GIRL: Oh.

PAUL: Two of 'em.

GIRL: Two wives.

PAUL: Yeah . . . I can tell you're kind of disappointed about it . . .

GIRL: *(Not terribly convincing:)* Nooo . . .

PAUL: It's okay to be disappointed! I'm disappointed with *myself!*

GIRL: Are you . . . ?

PAUL: I am. I mean, two wives is such a tiny number of wives.

GIRL: Excuse me?

PAUL: I know! It's unbelievable. All my buddies are always making fun of me at the gym:

(He recounts each of the jabs with frustrated disdain.)

"Hey, look over there — it's the guy with only two wives!"

"Maybe he wants a bite of my *Two*-nafish sandwich."

"He's like a ballerina with his *Two*-tu."

"I bet he likes the U.S. government, what with their *bicameral legislature.*"

"Hey everybody! Get your camera! It's a *TWO*-pac Shakur!"

or, y'know,

"Peace."

(He does an irritated impression of someone giving him the two-finger peace sign.)

I mean, *two* wives? *Two?* You gotta admit, that pretty pathetic. I'm embarrassed to show my face in public.

GIRL: Uh huh.

PAUL: And y'know, I'm thinking that you . . . *(Pause for effect.)* . . . *you* . . . might just be the perfect candidate for Numero Tres.

GIRL: I am . . .

PAUL: Absolutely!

GIRL: So you're Mormon?

PAUL: Mormon? No . . . Not Mormon.

GIRL: So why do you have two wives?

PAUL: Why? Why *not??*

GIRL: Well isn't polygamy illegal?

PAUL: What? Is it? I guess. *(Jovially dismissive:)* "Law"!

GIRL: Yes. Law.

PAUL: I mean, if everyone followed every itty bitty law, then you or I couldn't — I dunno — commit credit card identity theft.

GIRL: YES!

PAUL: What I'm saying is, everyone breaks the speed limit, right? I'm just breaking the speed limit with a bunch of different cars, simultaneously.

GIRL: That doesn't make any sense.

PAUL: Does the "Constitution" make sense?

GIRL: YES!

PAUL: So what do you think of my proposal? Be honest.

GIRL: Be honest?

PAUL: You wouldn't have a lot of responsibilities! Harriet is in charge of the cooking and cleaning, and Naomi takes the kids to soccer games and drama *(Rhymes with gamma.)* practice, so all I'd need from you is to Tivo my favorite shows for me while I'm at work, and then when I get home, occasionally shave my back.

GIRL: . . .

PAUL: *(Inviting.)* So . . . ?

(Pause. Girl decides to try a special angle.)

GIRL: All right, this is sounding like something I'd be interested in.

PAUL: Really?

GIRL: Yeah.

PAUL: For a second there I got the vibe there like you were freaked out.

GIRL: No no. Please. How could anyone be freaked out by anything you've said so far?

PAUL: That's what I'm saying!

GIRL: But there's one little thing you should know before we do this.

PAUL: Fire away!

GIRL: I have four husbands.

(Paul is expressionless.)

(Pause.)

(Pause.)

(Pause.)

PAUL: See that's just messed up.

(Blackout.)

END OF SCENE

The Dead Guy
Eric Coble

Comic
Eldon, twenties
Gina, thirties

Gina is producing the ultimate TV reality show. A contestant is given a huge amount of money and can spend it however he wishes for a week. When the week is over he is killed. She is trying to sell Eldon on becoming her first contestant.

(A bare stage with pieces of furniture representing different locations in the U.S. And there are two (or more) large TV monitors facing the audience. Currently they sit darkly quiet. At rise: A woman in a nice skirt, blouse and jacket, Gina, sits at a table with a 20-year-old man in jeans, T-shirt and flannel shirt. This is Eldon. They both have beers.)

GINA: No, seriously, I've had my eye on you for a while.

ELDON: You're shittin' me.

GINA: Check with the bartender. I was asking about you just an hour ago.

ELDON: But I wasn't here an hour ago.

GINA: I was asking him if he thought you'd be in.

ELDON: Me personally?

GINA: How many Eldon Phelps are there in Leadville?

ELDON: Just one. That I know about.

GINA: Exactly. *(Quietly, smiles.)* You've got quite a reputation in this town.

ELDON: Well, you know. Word gets around.

GINA: It certainly does. *(Beat. Eldon looks at her.)*

ELDON: You didn't talk to Jimmie Worley, did you? 'Cause you can't believe a word comes out of Jimmie Worley's mouth. That whole thing about me and his mother's Precious Moments figurines is total bullshit. He lies like a total lying sack of shit.

GINA: I haven't talked to Jimmie Worley.

ELDON: He's a lying sack of shit.

GINA: Okay.

ELDON: And don't talk to Brandon Chadwick either. Or Markie or Fritz or Darlene. Lying sacks of shit.

GINA: Some people —

ELDON: A guy can't catch a break, you know what I'm sayin'? This town is too small. It's like one grease fire and suddenly you're on everybody's shit list, you know?

GINA: I can imagine.

ELDON: And they found the goat in Brandon's basement, not mine. Brandon's. You ask anyone where the smell was coming from —

GINA: Eldon. I don't care about any of that. *(Quietly.)* I've got a proposition for you.

ELDON: *(Grins.)* Cool. You want to go back to my apartment? It's pretty clean.

GINA: I don't —

ELDON: And I got a little primo green left. I mean, there's not much, it's been a rough week, you know, but I'm willing to share, you know what I mean?

GINA: That's not what I mean. I want to help you. I know you've been going through a tough time.

ELDON: How'd you know that?

GINA: The people I've talked to. The bartender. Your ex-boss at the hardware store —

ELDON: He's a lying sack of shit.

GINA: I know. But the fact is you were fired. Am I right?

ELDON: See, I gotta get a lawyer for that. That's totally discrimination.

GINA: He claims you weren't coming in to work.

ELDON: See, that's what I mean, I'm not a morning person and I get penalized for that.

GINA: He says you were late eighteen of the twenty days you were scheduled.

ELDON: One of those times was the morning my car caught on fire.

GINA: Exactly —

ELDON: And two of those I was sick. It was Monday. I get sick on Monday mornings a lot —

GINA: Exactly. You've been sick, you have no car, you have no job —

ELDON: What are you, with the cops? 'Cause I was totally kidding about the primo weed. My apartment's empty — you ask anybody —

GINA: I'm not with the police. Although from what I can tell, you are about to be evicted.

ELDON: I gotta get a lawyer on that too. Do you know how many months behind on rent you have to be before they can legally kick you out?

GINA: My point is, things aren't going well for you.

ELDON: It's been a rough couple of weeks, yeah.

GINA: I'd like to help you turn things around.

ELDON: What. Like a lottery ticket?

GINA: Better. What do you want to do with your life?

ELDON: Get a new car.

GINA: And?

ELDON: Make Christy talk to me again.

GINA: Who's Christy?

ELDON: My girlfriend. My ex-girlfriend.

GINA: Good. What else?

ELDON: I like playing guitar.

GINA: What about the big picture?

ELDON: It'd be cool to be in a band again. Without Jimmie's mom having to drive us around.

GINA: I mean the big big picture. How do you want to be remembered?

ELDON: I don't know.

GINA: What do you want people to say about Eldon Phelps one hundred years from now?

ELDON: One hundred years? I don't know.

GINA: Imagine!

ELDON: I'd like 'em to say, "Damn, man, he was one of the greats. He totally had it goin' on."

GINA: And?

ELDON: "The world's a better place because of Eldon Phelps."

GINA: Yes! That's what I want to help you do. I want to help you make the world a better place and have the name Eldon Phelps go down in history.

ELDON: That doesn't sound too bad.

GINA: It sounds phenomenal. And I'm going to be the one to help you achieve it. I want to give you: One. Million. Dollars. To spend in any way you can dream of. *(She pulls a signed check from her purse and glides it in front of him.)*

ELDON: You're shittin' me.

GINA: I can do it. One million in your pocket. But you have to spend it all in one week.

ELDON: I could spend it in one day, dude! Right off, I'd replace all my Zeppelin CDs.

GINA: It has to last seven days. And you have to let me film you spending it.

ELDON: What?

GINA: I'm Gina Yaweth, Eldon.

ELDON: I'm Eldon Phelps, Gina. Should I have heard of you?

GINA: I produced "French Kiss".

ELDON: "French Kiss" . . .

GINA: The show about the five divorced pop stars who go to Paris to fight over one French hunk.

ELDON: Was that a reality show?

GINA: Totally real. And so is my new one running right now. It's called "Heavy Petting".

ELDON: Good title.

GINA: A group of contestants have to try to tame wild animals every week. Alligators, pythons, leopards — the winner gets a million and a new pet.

ELDON: And the losers get . . .

GINA: Stitches. Mechanical legs. It's not working out like we'd hoped.

ELDON: Jesus.

GINA: But not because of the injuries. Because of the ratings. We're tanking on Monday nights. That's why I need you.

ELDON: I don't do leopards, man. I'm, like, allergic to fur —

GINA: No leopards. Totally new show. The network's pulled the plug on "Heavy Petting" and I promised them I'd come up with something to fill the last week. To be perfectly honest with you Eldon, it's that or I'm out on my ass.

ELDON: I know the feeling.

GINA: And that's why I need Eldon Phelps. Reality TV is on its last legs, Eldon, it's wheezing and stumbling around blind, groping for any lifeline. It's time for you and me to send two million volts through its rotting flesh, my friend. On our show . . . we get to see how a totally ordinary, average nice guy who's never caught a break spends a million dollars —

ELDON: But it has to be spent in one week?

GINA: Seven days.

ELDON: What happens at the end of the week?

GINA: That's the hook of the show! At the end of the week . . . you die. *(Beat. He stares at her . . . then smiles.)*

ELDON: What. Like that's the — what do you call it — the idea, the premise. I'm going to die?

GINA: Except that it's real. You need to understand that. At the end of the week you will be legally obligated to truly, really die.

ELDON: Am I sick?

GINA: Not that I'm aware of. But that's the offer. No death, no money.

ELDON: But why —

GINA: Hear me out, Eldon, hear me out. I picked a spot on the map where I thought I'd find people having a hard time. Where I'd find — for want of a better word — losers. And I mean no offense by that. So I found Leadville. And when I arrived in Leadville yesterday, I started asking around about people in the county perceived, rightly or wrongly, as "losers." And your name came up. A lot. *(Eldon starts to speak.)* Which I don't agree with. Not at all. I'll tell you who the losers are, Eldon. It's the jealous, narrow-minded beetleheads who can't see who you really are, Eldon. And I am thanking God that I'm here to open their eyes. You have the personality, the charisma, the charm . . . and I have the money. Together we can blow this whole town — this whole country — wide open. BUT. The only way I can give you this money is if I get the ratings. And the only way I can get the ratings is to have something at stake, something never seen on any television. And that's a man who knows he only has seven days to live, but wants to go out with the biggest party, the most tears — someone about whom the world will say, "Damn, man, he was one of the greats, he had it goin' on! The world's a better place because of Eldon Phelps!"

ELDON: Yeah, but —

GINA: And I chose you, Eldon. Because, let's be honest, you're already at a dead end, am I right? In your heart, in your gut, you know it is not going to get any better than this. You can either drag yourself from day to day to day to day like the living dead for the rest of your meaningless life, leaving nothing behind but bad memories . . . or you can go out like a supernova, shining light to lead the world to a better, brighter tomorrow. And have one hell of a time doing it.

ELDON: But how would I die?

GINA: We don't know yet. That's part of the suspense. The viewers are going to choose.

ELDON: What?

GINA: We broadcast your adventures every day. At the end of each program, the audience gets to call in and vote on how you're going to die. If they like what they're seeing, they'll choose a sweet painless death. If they don't . . .

ELDON: I'm not doing leopards, man.

GINA: No leopards. I'll remove leopards from the list of options,

ELDON: *(Staring at her.)* Are you serious? Am I being punk'd, like I'm being filmed right now to see my reaction?

GINA: Not yet, you're not. But my camera man Dougie is waiting by the men's room. *(Holds out a contract.)* If you say yes, he'll start recording immediately.

ELDON: So I'd be on TV?

GINA: Every night for a week. It's going to be like nothing anyone's ever seen before — total cinema verité, no glamour, just grit and truth and reality. We only use one camera, natural light — we record your day and slam it together for broadcast at 9 p.m. every night. Monday through Sunday.

ELDON: So I'd go on a Sunday.

GINA: And it has to be next week. While we're still in Sweeps.

ELDON: Everyone would know who Eldon Phelps is. They'd know me.

GINA: On every lip. Living the American Dream.

ELDON: I could just go quick and painless?

GINA: I'll do my best. But it's up to the viewing public. I guess you'll have to ask yourself how much you trust the American people.

ELDON: So I could get a new car.

GINA: If that's what you want.

ELDON: Or a fleet of new cars? A different one for every day of the week! And I can go wherever I want —

GINA: Anywhere in the world, as long as Dougie follows you —

ELDON: I could do, like, anything!

GINA: *(Holding the check in front of his face . . .)* I'll give you everything you need, Eldon. The rest is up to you.

ELDON: Hell, yes.

END OF SCENE

Dog Sees God: Confessions of a Teenaged Blockhead

Bert V. Royal

Comic
Van's Sister & CB, both teens

Think of Van's Sister and CB as Lucy and Charlie Brown as teens. Lucy has become a pyromaniac and is incarcerated. Van comes to see her.

FIRE IS BAD

(Lights up on what looks like a booth. There is a chair facing it. Behind it sits Van's Sister. There's a sign at the corner of the booth that says: "The Doctor Is In." CB enters and Van's Sister smiles.

VAN'S SISTER: Well, it's about motherfucking time!

CB: Well, if a certain someone would stop getting thrown into solitary, then another certain someone could come visit more often.

VAN'S SISTER: *(Warmly.)* Sit down! Sit down!

CB: *(Reading the sign.)* "The Doctor Is In."

VAN'S SISTER: Boy, is she ever.

CB: Very funny.

VAN'S SISTER: I thought you might like it. How have you been? How is everybody?

CB: Everybody's pretty much the same. How are you?

VAN'S SISTER: I'm great. I'm doing really well. I've taken up knitting, I know that sounds cheesy, but it's been really good for me and I made you something! *(She holds up a scarf, but it's not nearly as interesting as the handcuffs that are restraining her hands.)*

CB: It's beautiful! Wow! Thanks. I'll wear it often. Don't the handcuffs seem a little unnecessary?

VAN'S SISTER: Are you kidding? I love them! They're kinky and you know me . . .

CB: I do.

VAN'S SISTER: *(Mockingly authoritative.)* Besides, it's for your protection.

CB: I'm not scared.

VAN'S SISTER: *(Grinning.)* Maybe you should be.

CB: When are you getting out of here already?

VAN'S SISTER: As soon as I can say three simple words: "Fire is bad." But I'm not in any hurry to rush out of here. They've got me on great drugs! Can I just say: I LOVE LITHIUM! You've gotta try it!

CB: Don't say shit like that. There are people who miss you out there.

VAN'S SISTER: Those people out there are just as crazy as the ones in here. *(She thinks on this.)* Did that sound cliché?

CB: Maybe not as much as "I love lithium."

VAN'S SISTER: I miss you!!! I think you should burn something down and you can join me here! We would have so much fun!

CB: Ugh! Fire. Is. Bad!

VAN'S SISTER: Ha ha. So, what's going on in your life?

CB: *(Blasé.)* Not much. I'm failing like three classes. I kissed Beethoven. And my sister's decided she's Wiccan this week. But that's just this week. I mean, she's gone completely —

VAN'S SISTER: WHAT?

CB: Wiccan. It's some sort of spooky goth thing. I don't really get it.

VAN'S SISTER: You kissed WHO?

CB: It wasn't a big deal. I kissed him last night at a party. In front of everybody. Although, it wasn't the first time.

VAN'S SISTER: Waitwaitwait. Slow down. Beethoven? Skinny, dorky Beethoven that we all make fun of?

CB: Yeah, the same one you were in love with.

VAN'S SISTER: When I was eight! This is a joke, right? My brother put you up to this, didn't he?

CB: Nope. True story.

VAN'S SISTER: Was it, like, a dare or something?

CB: No.

VAN'S SISTER: You just kissed him? Out of nowhere?

CB: Sort of.

VAN'S SISTER: And you're okay with this?

CB: I think so.

VAN'S SISTER: So?

CB: So?

VAN'S SISTER: So, what does this mean?

CB: I don't know.

VAN'S SISTER: Did you enjoy it?

CB: I wanted to do it.

VAN'S SISTER: Why?

CB: Because I felt like it.

VAN'S SISTER: Major parts of this story are missing, CB. What HAPPENED?

CB: Well, the first time we were in the music room.

VAN'S SISTER: At school?!

CB: Yeah, and we were talking. Actually we were fighting and then we were talking and I just kissed him.

VAN'S SISTER: And the second time?

CB: Party at Marcy's house.

VAN'S SISTER: And people saw?

CB: I wanted them to.

VAN'S SISTER: Oh my God. I don't believe this.

CB: Is it so hard to believe?

VAN'S SISTER: Yes!

CB: Why?

VAN'S SISTER: Because you did something different! You've always been so . . . predictable.

CB: Oh great. Here we go.

VAN'S SISTER: It's true! You know it's true. Kissing Beethoven is something that's so completely out of character for you. I mean, for a straight guy to kiss a gay guy — that's, like, something. That's . . . HOT!

CB: What if I'm not straight?

VAN'S SISTER: Are you coming out of the closet?

CB: I didn't say that.

VAN'S SISTER: But you didn't not say it either.

CB: Not not saying something isn't the same as saying something.

VAN'S SISTER: No offense, CB, but I don't think you're cool enough to be gay. Don't get me wrong, I love you to death, but if I had to imagine you giving a shit about home decoration or musical theatre, I just don't see it.

CB: Now you're using stereotypes.

VAN'S SISTER: Sorry, Miss Manners, but I'm in a bit of a shock right now.

CB: We had sex, too.

VAN'S SISTER: Ex-fucking-scuse me!?

CB: Yeah. After the party. We left and we had sex.

VAN'S SISTER: HOLY FUCKING SHIT!!! YOU'RE A HOMO, CB!!!

CB: Just because I did something that I wanted to do doesn't make me a homo. I've smoked pot. Doesn't mean I'm a pothead. I've drank plenty of beer. Doesn't make me a drunk. You set that little redheaded girl's hair on fire. Doesn't make you a pyromaniac.

VAN'S SISTER: *(Correcting him.)* Well, actually, technically it does.

CB: Okay. Bad example.

VAN'S SISTER: Are you going to do it again?

CB: I don't know. Maybe.

VAN'S SISTER: Do you have feelings for him?

CB: I don't know. I've grown up questioning everything I do. When we were kids, everybody — mostly YOU — told me what I was doing was wrong. It made me so self-conscious about everything. Good grief! It takes me an hour to get dressed every morning! I'm always thinking about what people are going to say or what they're going to think. And when I kissed him, I didn't care or wonder what anyone was going to think, I just did it.

VAN'S SISTER: That wasn't an answer. *(A silence passes.)*

CB: I can't stop thinking about him.

VAN'S SISTER: It sounds like love to me.

CB: What do I do?

VAN'S SISTER: You have to tell him.

CB: I can't.

VAN'S SISTER: Then resign yourself to being alone for eternity. That'll be five cents, please.

CB: I love it when we play doctor. *(She laughs.)*

VAN'S SISTER: *(Smiling.)* So, I guess this means we're not getting back together when I get out.

CB: Oh, so now you wanna get out of here, huh?

VAN'S SISTER: Fuck yeah! I didn't realize what I was missing! *(Beat.)* Oh, by the way. My brother told me about your dog. I'm really sorry. *(He had forgotten all about that.)*

CB: Oh. Yeah. Thanks.

VAN'S SISTER: It's a shame I'm locked up in here. We could've cremated him. *(He stares at her unimpressed.)* Sorry. Bad joke. *(A silence.)*

CB: Hey, why'd you do it?

VAN'S SISTER: What? Burn the bitch's hair off? Torch her tresses? Light her locks?

CB: Tell me.

VAN'S SISTER: Her hair is a symbol of innocence and my lighter is a symbol of corruption. God told me to do it. The devil made me do it. Charles Manson is just so damn persuasive. She is Joan of Arc and I am the townspeople of Salem. I did it for Jodie Foster! Boredom — plain and simple. It was a political statement! Allegorical! Metaphorical! A cry for help. A plea of insanity. *(Flexing her forefinger.)* Redrum! Redrum!

CB: Be serious!

VAN'S SISTER: Can't we just blame the government or the educational system? Puberty? P.M.S.? My parents?

CB: No.

VAN'S SISTER: Fine then. I did it because I felt like it.

CB: That's no excuse.

VAN'S SISTER: Really? You used it no less than five minutes ago.

CB: Public displays of affection and random acts of violence are two different things.

VAN'S SISTER: Are they? *(Beat.)* They say that love and hate are the closest two emotions.

CB: I'll bite. Why do you hate the little redheaded girl?

VAN'S SISTER: Because you used to love her.

CB: You did it because of me?

VAN'S SISTER: Yes. I just love you so intensely that it borderlines psychotic. You're all I ever think of.

CB: Seriously?

VAN'S SISTER: Nah, I'm just fucking with you. It's the lithium talking.

CB: *(Starting to stand.)* I'm gonna go now.

VAN'S SISTER: Wait! Don't! I was pregnant.

CB: Why can't you be honest with me like I've been with you?

VAN'S SISTER: I am. I was pregnant. *(Beat.)* Don't worry. It wasn't yours. I had just gotten an abortion the day before and the next day in Biology, we were ironically learning about reproduction. I'm listening to Miss Rainey talking about fallopian tubes, the uterus, eggs and I'm feeling sick to my stomach already. Trying to zone out on anything I can. So I start reading a note over Miss Puritanical Princess' shoulder and she's telling her friend *(Aping perfection.)* "how happy she is that she's a virgin and that she's going to stay that way until she gets married and how repulsed she is by all of the whores at our school." Without thinking, I reached into my pocket for my cute, little red Bic lighter and lit her cute, little red hair on fire. And every day in therapy, they ask me if I'm sorry yet and I just can't be. No matter how hard I try. Bitches like that make me sick. They've made me sick. I am officially sick, psychotic, unrepentant and unremorseful. I've been branded a sociopath and I have no choice but to believe it. *(CB smiles at her.)*

CB: Pregnant?

VAN'S SISTER: Pregnant.

CB: You're fucking with me again? *(She smiles. She pushes a button on her wrists and the cuffs fall off. She tosses the toy handcuffs aside. A buzz is heard.)* I gotta go. Visiting time is over.

VAN'S SISTER: I'm glad you came.

CB: Yeah, me too.

VAN'S SISTER: Before you go — I guess I don't have to ask how everyone reacted.

CB: To your incarceration?

VAN'S SISTER: I meant the kiss.

CB: Are you kidding? We hightailed it out of there so fast, I didn't even have time to look.

VAN'S SISTER: Smart kid.

CB: Although, I think my sister mouthed "I hope you die" at me across the breakfast table this morning. But the clock is ticking and I guess I'll find out how everybody else votes tomorrow at school.

VAN'S SISTER: Good luck.

CB: Thanks.

VAN'S SISTER: CB, I'm so proud of you for breaking through. For setting one foot outside the norm and giving no apologies. Promise me that you won't apologize.

CB: I won't.

VAN'S SISTER: I have faith in you. *(They embrace.)* And next time when you come, if you could just maybe stick a book of matches up your ass, I'd be your best friend forever. *(CB gets up and leaves, but not before saying —)*

CB: *(Smiling.)* You already are. *(Lights out. In darkness —)*

VAN'S SISTER: Hey, Blockhead! You forgot your scarf! *(The sound of a cell door closing.)*

END OF SCENE

Levittown

Marc Palmieri

Dramatic
Kevin Briggs (mid to late twenties or thirty)
Colleen Briggs (early to mid twenties)

Colleen and Kevin are brother and sister. Their mother recently moved, with Colleen, back into her childhood home in Levittown, Long Island, where her father, a World War II veteran, still lives. Colleen has had a history of drug and alcohol abuse, but has, for some two years, remained clean. She is a nursing student at a local college. Kevin is also a college student, but has recently dropped out of his fourth school. Colleen has just picked him up from the airport. Their abusive father, divorced from their mother for many years, lives a half hour away. Colleen and her father have not spoken in six years.

(The Maddigan home. It is the year 1999. The living room of a classic Levitt house on Long Island. There is a sofa, a well-worn reading chair, two open doorways that lead to separate areas of the home; one upstage left to the kitchen at the front of the house and one upstage right to a hall. The front door is stage left. Stairs sit extreme stage right ascending to the upper floor beyond view. On the sofa, a coffee table, and elsewhere about the room are large paperback books, some alone, some in stacks. Upstage there is a brick wall between the doorways, which separates the living room and the kitchen. The walls are sporadically adorned with photographs of children in all phases of life, and of a World War II soldier with his bride. Over the mantel of the brick wall hangs a large, prominent, fireman's helmet on an oak-based memorial plaque. At rise: Keys are heard opening the lock of the front door. It opens and Colleen Briggs (twenties), her brother Kevin, her elder by 3 years, enter, in mid-conversation. He carries a suitcase.)

KEVIN: It's not that anything was wrong with the place. That's not what I mean.

COLLEEN: You just didn't like it?

KEVIN: No, I did.

COLLEEN: Did you like the teachers?

KEVIN: Oh, they were great professors. I was getting good work done, the classes were great, the campus is beautiful. It was . . . I don't know. I can't explain it. And anyway what do you do with a major in History?

COLLEEN: There's lots you can do. You want water?

(Colleen exits to the kitchen.)

KEVIN: Sure. Thanks.

(A beat. Kevin looks around the room.)

I don't know. I know I want to learn. I just don't know what. It didn't feel right so, why stay any longer than I have to? Anyway, how is *this?* You guys living here now. This all happened so fast.

COLLEEN: *(Re-entering.)* Well it made sense I guess. Mom's been driving forty minutes here every day for years to visit Gramps. Figured it was better to just move in.

KEVIN: I want to drive by the old house later.

COLLEEN: I wouldn't call it old. We just moved out a month ago.

KEVIN: Yeah but it's now our *old* house. I wasn't even there to —

COLLEEN: To what, say goodbye? Come on, man. We went through hell in that house. Don't act like you miss it.

KEVIN: Who bought it?

COLLEEN: A little happy yuppie family. I drove by once or twice. Morbid curiosity. Tried to get myself to go cry over it or something. I parked across the street, stared at it. There's one of those huge plastic jungle gyms on the lawn. Fisher Price. These dorks were actually standing there, by the front door, his arm around her waist, watching their kids run around playing. Figured *that* would hit me, right? A brother and sister? After awhile I thought, why the hell am I doing this? I don't miss this place. Goodbye.

KEVIN: So where are you staying? Upstairs?

COLLEEN: Yup. Those rooms are weird up there. Ceiling is sloped with the roof. If you sit up fast in bed you bust your head. The other room's for you. Uncle Jack's old room. There's a bed in there. If you can get to it. Room's full of boxes.

KEVIN: Of what?

COLLEEN: I don't know. Old stuff. Mom's and Uncle Jack's clothes, school stuff, albums, you know.

KEVIN: Where's Mom sleep?

COLLEEN: *(Points toward the hall.)* In her old room. Imagine being in your fifties and moving back into your room?

KEVIN: Where is everybody?

COLLEEN: They're at that class.

KEVIN: God, I can't believe she drags Gramps to that.

COLLEEN: Old people yoga. Twelve weeks of sitting on mats while some eunuch from the Hamptons reads poems over a woodwind CD. Friggin' quacks. Sorry. I can't help it. An entire cultural movement based on the miracles of stress reduction, and one of its great enthusiasts lives right here, driving me fuckin' nuts. I had more fun in withdrawal.

KEVIN: Coll!

COLLEEN: Look at this. Every week there's a new Earth-shattering revelation at Barnes & Noble.

(She picks up some books.)

The Open Leaf, The Flowing Bliss . . . kiss my ass.

KEVIN: Well maybe it's good for him.

COLLEEN: Doubt it.

KEVIN: Well I'm sure he loves having you guys. He's been alone here.

COLLEEN: Yeah, kind of. Though he talks to himself. Talks to Grandma actually.

KEVIN: What do you mean?

COLLEEN: I caught him when I came home late one night. Right here in his chair. Freaked me out. Says he's been doing it for years. Talks to Grandma like she's still here. Yesterday morning he had an argument with her about the coffee maker.

(A beat. Kevin laughs.)

He can hardly walk now. Legs are really bad. Mom actually told him it was "stress" not shrapnel.

(A beat.)

So what do you want to do?

KEVIN: Right now?

COLLEEN: I mean, next. Are you gonna go to another school? There's got to be some subject you haven't tried.

KEVIN: I don't know. You know, I'm thinking I might . . .

(A beat.)

Let me get some more water.

COLLEEN: I'll get it. Sit down.

(She takes his glass, exits. Kevin looks around again.)

KEVIN: You know, I think my oldest memories are in this house. This door wasn't here. It was a window. Wow. Everything was in this room. Christmas. Gramps, Mom, Grandma on the couch.

COLLEEN: That old dog that would just moan.

KEVIN: Bo. I remember Uncle Jack tickling the hell out of him and Grandma yelling at him to "stahhp it!"

COLLEEN: *(Re-entering.)* I don't remember Uncle Jack.

KEVIN: I remember him a little. Right here, holding Joey. And how about the Lynch twins down the street, remember them? Their father was a Nassau cop. Nearly every time we'd visit I'd end up playing with them. It was horrible.

COLLEEN: Why?

KEVIN: The Lynch twins would find me in the backyard here and tell me I had sixty seconds to hide.

COLLEEN: Hide n' seek?

KEVIN: They called it, "Hide, seek and force a confession." Those were tough girls.

(A beat. They laugh.)

But I should've come here to visit more often . . . this is an amazing place. Levittown is an amazing place.

COLLEEN: I hadn't noticed.

KEVIN: This whole town was like a dream. It *was* a dream. Or many dreams. Bill Levitt. He built thousands of these houses on scrap left over from the war. We just studied this! My own grandparents' home, my mother's home, and I knew nothing about it! Had to learn it from Professor Mirsky in "Political and Social History of Postwar America." That's when I realized how little I know about myself. My own . . . everything. Family, history. Do you even know what Grandma's maiden name was?

COLLEEN: It was an Italian name. Lah — something?

KEVIN: Or where they lived before this? Or where Grandpa was in the war?

COLLEEN: He was a cook in the army. Brooklyn? Didn't they live in Brooklyn?

KEVIN: I don't know. And he was a cook but he has shrapnel in his leg! How did that happen? Or, what was Mom like as a kid? Where was Grampa's firehouse? What do I need school and degrees for? What I really should learn about is right here in this house. Up there in those boxes!

COLLEEN: Well, it's a small house. Joe Levitt —

KEVIN: Bill Levitt.

COLLEEN: Yeah. His houses are too small. Can't get away from anyone.

KEVIN: They didn't want to. I mean, they did, but not from their families. That was the point. This room here? This room was a whole concept in itself. The family room. The common space they could share. Grow up together. And it's furthest from the street, see? Where the man could come home every day and forget the world, the war, work . . . put everything behind him.

(A beat.)

Anyway, how are you doing?

COLLEEN: Okay.

KEVIN: How are you doing . . . with everything?

COLLEEN: Good.

KEVIN: You know I . . . this sounds strange to say but I'm actually thrilled to see you chubby.

COLLEEN: Oh yeah?

KEVIN: No. No. You're not chubby. You're very skinny. You know what I mean —

COLLEEN: I know. You're hilarious.

KEVIN: Coll?

COLLEEN: Yeah.

KEVIN: You . . .

(A beat.)

COLLEEN: What?

KEVIN: You look very good.

COLLEEN: I look normal and healthy. And I am. Thank you.

(A beat.)

KEVIN: Things are good?

COLLEEN: *(Smiling.)* Yes, things are good.

(A beat.)

Nothing, really.

KEVIN: What nothing?

COLLEEN: Nothing's new.

KEVIN: I didn't ask that.

COLLEEN: Oh. Hah. Well, woops.

(A beat.)

KEVIN: What's the matter with you?

COLLEEN: I haven't talked to you much the past few months.

KEVIN: I know. I mean, I took that as a good thing. I mean —

COLLEEN: It was. See, Kev, living in this fascinating historic house has gotten me so in touch with myself. Healed all the wounds in my soul. I'm an "Open Leaf."

KEVIN: You're flowing bliss!

COLLEEN: Yes! But it's something else, too.

KEVIN: What else?

(A beat.)

COLLEEN: There's this man I met. And he's the best person I've ever known. And now he wants to marry me.

(Silence.)

KEVIN: *(Stunned.)* Are you kidding?

COLLEEN: I've played it way down. I didn't want to . . . I don't know. His name is Brian. I told Gramps he proposed but nobody else. They've only met him a couple times.

KEVIN: Why haven't I heard about this? How long have you been with him?

COLLEEN: I don't know. Five, six months or so.

KEVIN: Five months, and nobody told me? You never told me? Marriage?

COLLEEN: Yup.

KEVIN: Jesus. When?

COLLEEN: When did he say it?

KEVIN: Or when . . . yeah! When did he say it?

COLLEEN: Three weeks ago tomorrow.

KEVIN: And what did you say —

COLLEEN: I said yes.

KEVIN: Oh my God. Are you serious?

COLLEEN: Yes.

KEVIN: I'm . . . I'm happy! Right? I'm supposed to be happy?

COLLEEN: *(Laughing.)* Yes. You are.

(They hug.)

KEVIN: Who is he? I mean —

COLLEEN: You'll meet him. You'll like him. And look, you and Gramps are the only ones who know right now. He's coming over Friday and we'll announce it all together nice and dorky for Mom.

KEVIN: Oh, Coll. Does Dad know?

(Pause.)

COLLEEN: No. How would he know?

KEVIN: I . . . I don't know.

(A beat.)

Can I tell him?

(A pause.)

COLLEEN: I'm very glad you're happy for me.

KEVIN: Of course I am.

COLLEEN: And I wish I could say yes, that I want you to tell him. But I have to say, don't tell him.

(She lifts her hand, he sees a ring.)

Look at this.

KEVIN: Ah, it's beautiful, Coll. Oh my God. Did you have this on all that time, and I didn't notice?

COLLEEN: No. It was in my pocket. I keep it in my pocket.

KEVIN: Why don't you wear it?

COLLEEN: I don't know. It's the most beautiful thing I've ever seen. And I feel better when it's off.

KEVIN: I think he'd prefer you kept it on.

COLLEEN: I do when I'm around him. And when I sleep. It feels perfect then. Yeah.

END OF SCENE

Life Science

Anna Ziegler

Dramatic
Tom & Leah, teens

Tom and Leah are on the second date. On their first date Leah talked a lot — about her fears of another Holocaust, about her mother, about not wanting to drink alone. So now, Tom is drinking with her and they're kissing for the first time.

(Tom and Leah make out on the couch. On the coffee table sit a number of beer bottles, all empty.)

LEAH: *(Quietly.)* Oh Tom.

TOM: Yeah?

LEAH: No — I was saying it for emphasis. Like "oh that was nice."

TOM: Oh . . . Good.

LEAH: Yeah, good.

(More making out.)

TOM: Leah?

LEAH: Uh-huh?

TOM: Can I?

LEAH: Uh-huh.

(He takes off her shirt and stares at her chest; moments pass slowly.)

TOM: Wow. Thanks.

LEAH: You're not supposed to say that. Not out loud.

TOM: I'm not?

LEAH: There are some rules, I think.

(She moves farther down the couch and covers her chest.)

TOM: Like what?

LEAH: I don't know. There's something about killing the mood. You're not supposed to do that.

TOM: Maybe I should put on some music?

LEAH: Yeah, that might work.

(He stands and turns on the stereo. Totally inappropriate music blares — Gregorian Chant or Carmina Burana or something. Tom quickly turns it off.)

TOM: Sorry about that.

LEAH: Is there anything else?

TOM: Maybe the radio.

(He turns it on. Commercials. More commercials. He turns it off. Leah puts her shirt back on.)

LEAH: You don't have any other CDs down here?

TOM: My parents keep most of them in the car. For trips, you know.

LEAH: They go away a lot, huh.

TOM: Yeah, I guess.

LEAH: Why? Don't they love you?

TOM: I'm sorry?

LEAH: I mean, don't they care that you're growing up and one day soon you won't be here anymore?

TOM: You make it sound like I'm dying or something.

LEAH: My mom gets all emotional all the time these days when she sees me like looking at colleges online or studying for the SATs. She comes up to me and hugs me and won't let me go because soon I'll be gone and there will only be memories.

TOM: But isn't your brother, like, younger than you?

LEAH: Yeah, but I'm the girl, like it's a mother-daughter thing. Dylan doesn't talk to her about menopause and that disease you can get from tampons and stuff.

TOM: I hope not.

LEAH: But I can. It's a mother-daughter thing. I guess your mom never had that with anyone.

TOM: She had it with her mom.

LEAH: I mean, not having a daughter or anything.

TOM: I guess not.

LEAH: Do you ever wish you had siblings?

TOM: I don't know, I —

LEAH: I mean, does it get lonely?

TOM: Not really.

LEAH: Do you ever think that you might have siblings out there, somewhere?

TOM: What?

LEAH: I mean, that you have a brother or a sister or lots of brothers and sisters and they could just be like walking all around you; they could be at RHS for God's sake — and you wouldn't even know it?

TOM: I don't think they're at RHS.

LEAH: Why not?

TOM: Well there are only two other Asian kids in the school and they're Chinese and Japanese.

LEAH: So?

TOM: So I'm not Chinese or Japanese.

LEAH: You're not?

TOM: No.

LEAH: Well they could be at other schools, like in Bethesda or Chevy Chase or . . .

TOM: Leah.

LEAH: Yeah?

TOM: My life is . . . my life. You know?

LEAH: Not really, but okay.

TOM: I mean, it is what it is.

LEAH: Okay.

TOM: It's not . . . something I think about.

LEAH: So you said.

TOM: Anyway . . . aren't your . . . don't your parents wonder where you are?

LEAH: I told them I was staying over at Dana's.

TOM: Oh. Okay.

LEAH: So. That's not a problem.

TOM: Right.

LEAH: Anyway, she's like obsessed these days with this idea. She's not really fun to be around.

TOM: I thought you never had fun with her.

LEAH: I've known her since second grade. It's complicated.

TOM: I'm sorry — I didn't mean to suggest that —

LEAH: And now she wants to adopt this boy *Abdul* from Lebanon.

(Beat.)

TOM: Is that a joke?

LEAH: No. I don't think so.

TOM: She can't adopt anyone.

LEAH: I know. And I mean, *Abdul?* First of all, that means, like, descendent of Allah or something. And second, Israelis killed his parents. If he didn't hate the Jews before, there's no way he doesn't now.

TOM: She's not old enough to adopt anyone.

LEAH: He's probably already signed up with Hezbollah.

TOM: Leah.

LEAH: Yeah?

TOM: Come back over here.

LEAH: Why don't you come over here?

(Tom does. He puts his arm around Leah. She studies him.)

LEAH: Has anyone ever told you that you look a little . . . I mean, young for your age?

TOM: Why, how young do I look?

LEAH: I feel like you could be . . . I don't know . . . fourteen.

TOM: Fourteen!

LEAH: Is that bad?

TOM: It's not good.

LEAH: I guess not. No.

(Beat.)

TOM: That wasn't a very nice thing to say.

LEAH: I'm sorry. *(Beat.)* How old do you think I look? I mean, how old could I pass for?

TOM: I don't know. I think you look your age.

LEAH: Really? Not even a year older? I look in the mirror and I feel nineteen.

TOM: You don't look nineteen.

LEAH: Eighteen?

TOM: I don't know. I guess.

LEAH: When I straighten my hair, I look at least twenty.

TOM: Sure.

LEAH: Does Mike think I look . . . my age?

TOM: I've never discussed it with him.

LEAH: Huh.

TOM: Should I have?

LEAH: You do play soccer together, don't you?

TOM: Yeah.

LEAH: Do you ever like talk to each other?

TOM: I don't know. Sometimes.

LEAH: Okay.

TOM: I mean, Mike's parents are crazy. Come to all the games. Yell at him. His dad's embarrassing. We can all hear him.

LEAH: Do your parents do that?

TOM: Oh no. Well. they don't come to too many games.

LEAH: Oh.

(They look at each other. Leah leans in and kisses Tom.)

LEAH: Did you know, you kind of . . . no offense or anything, but you kind of kiss like a fish?

TOM: *(Quietly.)* What?

LEAH: That's what it feels like. Like I'm in a fish tank surrounded by water.

TOM: I don't even know what means . . . but it doesn't sound good.

LEAH: No, I wouldn't call it good. It felt a little . . . inexperienced.

TOM: Great.

LEAH: Have you ever . . . I mean, have you ever done this before?

TOM: Has anyone ever told you you're pretty blunt?

LEAH: My mother's incredibly blunt. It gets her in trouble sometimes.

TOM: Yeah, well.

(Beat.)

No I haven't. I mean, not with someone like you.

LEAH: I mean, not counting spin the bottle or anything. Because I know you probably like kissed Rachel Targoff because everyone like kissed Rachel Targoff because she was the only one to play those stupid debasing games.

TOM: Yeah, I kissed her.

LEAH: But it doesn't count.

TOM: Whatever. Look.

LEAH: I mean, I'm not trying to hurt you. I'm trying to like, help. We could improve.

(Tom stands abruptly and runs offstage. Sounds of vomiting. Leah doesn't move. The toilet flushes. In a few moments, Tom returns. He sits down next to her.)

Ew.

TOM: I feel better now.

LEAH: Great.

(Beat.)

So where do you think your top college choices are?

TOM: *(Shocked she could ask him that now.)* I don't know.

LEAH: Listen . . . can I be frank with you?

TOM: It won't be the first time.

LEAH: I think we should go out. Neither of us has . . . dated anyone seriously yet and it's senior year and I think we'd be a good match. Good enough at least. I mean, it's not gonna be forever; it's just gonna be a year and then we'll go our separate ways.

TOM: Um . . . I don't —

LEAH: There's a certain logic to it, Tom.

TOM: There is?

LEAH: My parents had an arranged marriage. Can you believe that? A matchmaker named Lucy Brownstein, who lived in this like basement in Staten Island found them for each other. It cost one thousand dollars. So compared to that, this is nothing.

TOM: But, with things that are arranged, someone outside does the arranging.

LEAH: What are you saying? You don't want to go out with me?

(She looks down.)

TOM: No. I . . . I just don't feel like . . . I mean . . . I just threw up. I'm feeling a little . . . well, light-headed or something.

(He puts his head back on the cushion.)

LEAH: Do you want me to read to you? That sounds like a romantic thing to do. Sometimes my dad reads to my mom, when her eyes are tired and she doesn't want to read anymore.

TOM: No. I'm fine.

LEAH: I can, though.

(She takes out Alan Dershowitz's 'The Case for Israel.')

TOM: Don't.

LEAH: My only concern is that, even though you're Jewish, you're not *really* Jewish, you know? My parents are apprehensive about diluting the race too much.

TOM: Leah?

LEAH: Yes?

TOM: This is all . . . I'm feeling a little . . . wiped out, really.

LEAH: I think your parents really leave you alone too often. It seems like you need some TLC.

TOM: No, I really —

LEAH: It's good for hangovers too. Maybe it could ward one off.

TOM: I don't have a hangover. I'm still . . . drunk.

(He closes his eyes.)

LEAH: Tom, I like you. Don't go to sleep.

TOM: I have to.

LEAH: Please.

(Silence.)

Tom?

(Silence, then she whispers.)

I feel lonely. And you're not supposed to be lonely when you're with someone else — the person you love, or are dating, or are about to be dating. But I do, Tom, I feel all alone. Someday soon there's gonna be a religious war and I'm gonna be stuck in an attic somewhere, without very much food or even a pen to write with, and I'm going to remember this moment when you left me alone, needlessly, selfishly. And I'm going to stare out the tiny window that's really too dirty to see out of and for a second I'll think I'm seeing the sky and a bird. Just that and it will be the happiest moment. Like a huge meal, or a big open field. And I'll wish I could share it with you, Tom. Or maybe with Mike. But probably with you.

(She kisses him on the cheek and lies down beside him.)

END OF SCENE

Manuscript

Paul Grellong

Dramatic

Elizabeth & David, late teens

David has invited Chris over to his parents' home during winter break. He has arrived with his new girlfriend Elizabeth. Chris has left to go get the drugs for the evening leaving Elizabeth and David. It turns out they have a secret shared history.

ELIZABETH: Before you say anything —

DAVID: Fuck you.

ELIZABETH: Real writers don't need to use profanity to express anger.

DAVID: How dare you come into my house. And this "perfect strangers" act for Chris' benefit, I'm gonna be sick.

ELIZABETH: I'm having fun with it. You know you are, too, don't lie. You're on fire tonight.

DAVID: I want you out of here now.

ELIZABETH: How's Harvard so far? Is it totally boring?

DAVID: This is my *room.* Get out.

ELIZABETH: But I just got here.

DAVID: *(Pause.)* You ended up at Yale?

ELIZABETH: Oh, bullshit, like you didn't know exactly where I went to college?

DAVID: It may come as a surprise to you that not everyone follows the intricate details of your life.

ELIZABETH: Of course they don't. But I know you do.

DAVID: You're wrong. And Chris tells me about his new girl friend, her name is Elizabeth. Now, see, the back-stabbing hellcat from my past went by "Liz," so how was I supposed to know?

ELIZABETH: You really aren't happy to see me at all.

DAVID: Not in the least.

ELIZABETH: You're a good actor.

DAVID: Oh, please. You deserve an Oscar for the shit you were slinging earlier.

ELIZABETH: "I want to thank my fans, this is for all my wonderful fans."

DAVID: He has no idea that we know each other.

ELIZABETH: And I want to keep it that way. Chris is a good kid.

DAVID: "Good kid"? He's six months older than both of us.

ELIZABETH: You know what I mean. He's not old inside like us.

DAVID: What? You're insane. How could you not tell him about the journalism program, how we —

ELIZABETH: At first? Because I wanted to sleep with him. I recognized him right away . . . your pictures on the wall that summer, I have a good memory. So there we are, it's a party, it's late, things are going well. I thought I was in for a one-night stand, if I was in for anything at all. Then later he finds out who I am to you, things blow up, everyone moves on: We're *adults.* But things never blew up.

DAVID: I didn't tell him.

ELIZABETH: Clearly.

DAVID: I never told anyone. It was embarrassing for me.

ELIZABETH: "Embarrassing."

DAVID: That was my article.

ELIZABETH: Funny, I could have sworn I saw my name underneath the title.

DAVID: What a joke.

ELIZABETH: No, I'm being serious. Right between the "by" and the first word of the piece.

DAVID: That was the most heartless thing I have ever seen.

ELIZABETH: I like to set records. Sue me.

DAVID: "Sue you."

ELIZABETH: Which you never did. It wouldn't have been airtight, anyway, so that was probably wise on your part.

DAVID: I talked to my parents about it, they were the only ones. They asked me: If I was gonna be a writer, was that really how I wanted to get started? Did I want always be known as That Kid from the Lawsuit? I thought about it, decided: No, that wasn't what I wanted. I'd write something else. I'd get a second chance. All of which you'd know if you ever answered one of my phone calls last year.

ELIZABETH: Water under the bridge? What do you say?

DAVID: I can't believe what you've been doing to him.

ELIZABETH: Hang on. I like him. I do. But I missed you.

DAVID: Yeah, right.

ELIZABETH: Hey, it surprised me, too. But I really wanted to see you again. I knew it would be fun, but not *this* fun.

DAVID: You're in my home . . .

ELIZABETH: David, honey, I've been planning this for longer than you think. *(Beat.)*

DAVID: I thought I was going to fall over. When you walked in. I —

ELIZABETH: You played it off. Admirably. I admired you.

DAVID: You're a sick person.

ELIZABETH: A part of me thought you might have figured it out. Every day that went by and Chris didn't come to me with, "Who the hell are you? You're a thief and all the rest of the blah blah blah," that was me getting one day closer to you. *(Pause.)* I thought maybe you were keeping it from him, too. That it was a game we were playing. I liked playing it.

DAVID: There wasn't any game. If I had figured it out, you'd have known it.

ELIZABETH: Ooh. Listen to you . . .

DAVID: What are you doing here?

ELIZABETH: It would have been nice to meet Banks, but seeing you again is the main thing.

DAVID: Why do you want to see me? I don't want to see you.

ELIZABETH: To thank you.

DAVID: You want to thank me.

ELIZABETH: I want to say something: Thank you.

DAVID: Go fuck yourself.

ELIZABETH: The customary response is "you are welcome" . . . however, given the circumstances, I accept your version.

DAVID: And, so, here we are. *(Pause.)* How's the publishing business?

ELIZABETH: Good. It misses you. Oh, no, wait . . .

DAVID: First of all: I was writing about my experience at Exeter. You take it, you make it about St. Paul's by, what, changing the names of the dining hall and some neighboring towns?

ELIZABETH: Yes.

DAVID: That should never have worked! Exeter and St. Paul's are completely different.

ELIZABETH: Not really.

DAVID: Are you crazy? Of course they are! Com*pletely* different! That's like, they're not even like apples and oranges, they're like . . . apples and *station* wagons.

ELIZABETH: Are you listening to yourself? Because you should.

DAVID: At the risk of sounding blurb-y: I was writing about my experience, that of a young, Jewish male going to a WASP-y fucking prep school.

ELIZABETH: Oh, and your language was so beautiful. Just like now.

DAVID: And you *stole* it! You rewrote it and made it about being a girl! You kept all of the good stuff — okay, you changed the title — but you stole the structure and you changed the main thing.

ELIZABETH: So?

DAVID: Thematically speaking, "Jews" and "girls" are not the same!

ELIZABETH: What about Jewish girls?

DAVID: Don't be sly.

ELIZABETH: "Sly"? Who are you, Charles Dickens?

DAVID: Our articles — or, I should say, my article and your version of my article . . . they're not the same.

ELIZABETH: You're right. Mine's better.

DAVID: Hardly. You couldn't even plagiarize right.

ELIZABETH: There were enough thematic similarities to make the rewrite less than difficult. My version is more smooth.

DAVID: "Smooth"? What the fuck is "smooth"?

ELIZABETH: To tell the truth, the hardest part was combing through it and changing the voice of an adolescent boy into that of a — gosh, someone wrote in, they published that letter the next week, what did it say again? Oh, yes: "This young lady is a true, good writer, just this side of greatness."

DAVID: Yawn. You're about as ladylike as my uncle Phil.

ELIZABETH: But look at this dress.

DAVID: *(Pacing; practically ranting.) Fuck* the dress. Sir Walter Raleigh would have kept his cloak on, laid you down in the puddle and stepped across via the small of your back. Ladylike, indeed. *(Beat.)*

ELIZABETH: You look good.

DAVID: What?

ELIZABETH: College has been good for you. I like your hair longer.

DAVID: Oh, yeah? Could you hand me the scissors? Right there on the desk . . .

ELIZABETH: Where's my book?

DAVID: Come again?

ELIZABETH: You don't have my book on the shelf.

DAVID: I don't have your book at all.

ELIZABETH: Bullshit.

DAVID: I don't have time to read books. I just read the *Book Review.*

ELIZABETH: It's the same thing.

DAVID: Isn't it?

ELIZABETH: But I know you've got the book.

DAVID: You think I'd read your book?

ELIZABETH: Cover to cover.

DAVID: Okay, this has been super. Thanks for stopping by. I'll tell Chris you were feeling sick or something.

ELIZABETH: You can't shake me. You should be so lucky.

DAVID: I can't believe you're in my house. I can't believe you would *come* to my *home.*

ELIZABETH: I am. And I did! Oh, Davey, you have no idea how happy it makes me to see your befuddled little face. It's been a long time since I've had that pleasure.

DAVID: Relax, it's been a year.

ELIZABETH: Seems like longer.

DAVID: I've tried to block it all out many a time.

ELIZABETH: I guess. But, still, I couldn't have done it without you.

DAVID: Excuse me?

ELIZABETH: Let's agree on one thing: I wrote a good book. Let's agree on another: I might never have had it published if it wasn't for the article.

DAVID: *My* article.

ELIZABETH: Stay with me: You can plant a flag wherever you want in this, but think about it: *Your* article never would have made it out of the slush pile. You couldn't have done it without me, either.

DAVID: You're a thief.

ELIZABETH: No, I'm not. I *rewrote* that shit. I was a facilitator. And I don't need to facilitate anymore. I've got an agent now, I got a two-book deal. I'm home free. I'm going to college on a fucking *lark,* Yale's English department, the *parties* are good, you think otherwise I'd hang out in New Haven? Talk about fucking armpits . . .

DAVID: For your information, New Haven has many underappreciated sites of beauty.

ELIZABETH: Name one. *(No response.)* You're still an idiot.

DAVID: You're still a snake bitch.

ELIZABETH: I don't *want* to be calling you names, but they're screaming out to be called, David. You never did know when to keep your mouth shut, when to trust people . . .

DAVID: I learned the hard way with you.

ELIZABETH: But that was just stupid. Half of me took your article on principle.

DAVID: But I shared it with you. I wanted your feedback.

ELIZABETH: You don't hand over something that good like it's a shopping list or a *baseball card.* You have a piece like that, you better sit on it until someone snatches it up.

DAVID: Someone did.

ELIZABETH: You know what I mean.

DAVID: You told me to wait. You told me I had to submit it after graduation, just *had* to. That way it would be more commercial, more readable, if high school was over and done with. So, I *did* sit on it. I *did* keep working on it in private, like you said. Because I believed you.

ELIZABETH: And so you learned. I did you a favor of galactic proportions. *(Beat.)*

DAVID: You don't even have a second book.

ELIZABETH: I'm in no rush.

DAVID: You'll never, no matter how hard you try, you'll never be your sister.

ELIZABETH: Who wants to be her? She's a hyper-realist.

DAVID: *(Pause.)* I called you. And wrote to you. Why didn't you —

ELIZABETH: David. Really.

DAVID: I was young.

ELIZABETH: It was a *year* ago. You wanted to *fuck* me.

DAVID: That's a laugh.

ELIZABETH: You still want to fuck me.

DAVID: I want to do something to you, but I'm not sure that's it.

ELIZABETH: You shouldn't be mad anymore. You should have channeled all of this a long time ago.

DAVID: "It was a year ago."

ELIZABETH: Now you're stealing from me. Copycat.

DAVID: When's your boyfriend coming back? *(David goes to the window.)*

ELIZABETH: Never. You're stuck here with me for the whole night.

DAVID: Could be worse.

ELIZABETH: How's that?

DAVID: Could be for two nights. *(Looks out the window.)* He's coming up the block now. So, listen, it was good, it was great, it was thrilling to see you again . . .

ELIZABETH: You're speaking like the evening's over.

DAVID: A boy can dream, can't he?

ELIZABETH: Settle in. This night has only just begun. *(Elizabeth walks over to David seductively. She is gorgeous. David can't deny it. He squirms slightly.)* David. Do you want to kiss me or hit me?

DAVID: Both. *(Elizabeth leans in and kisses David full on the mouth. He kisses back. They grab at each other forcefully, kissing hard. Then she pulls back. She stands in front of him and waits.)*

ELIZABETH: Well? *(Beat.)* You pussy. *(From off, we hear the front door open and close.)*

DAVID: How do you know I won't tell him everything right now, right now when he walks in?

ELIZABETH: Because this is that game. Because playing it is turning you on.

END OF SCENE

The Mistakes Madeline Made

Elizabeth Meriwether

Comic
Edna, twenty-one
Buddy, late twenties

Edna suffers from Ablutophobia, the fear of bathing. Buddy is a guy in a crumpled suit.

BUDDY: YOU CAN COME IN, SARAH! *(To Edna.)* Tell her she can come in! I'LL CLOSE MY EYES SARAH!

EDNA: Shut up, shut up, shut up —

BUDDY: Sarah came in here like ten times today —

EDNA: It's the bathroom! Buddy, you have to . . . um. Sarah's my roommate and she's just trying to use the bathroom? We're, like, in the middle of midterms?

BUDDY: Why does she look at me like that?

EDNA: *(Whispered.)* She has a lazy eye. *(Slight pause.)*

BUDDY: OH SARAH, LET'S PUT THAT LAZY EYE TO WORK!

EDNA: Oh my God, oh my God, oh my God —

BUDDY: I LOVE YOU JUST THE WAY YOU ARE, SARAH!

EDNA: *(Overlapping.)* I CAN HANDLE THIS, SARAH, I'M A PEER HEALTH EDUCATOR! She's gone. Buddy —

BUDDY: You're a peer health educator?

EDNA: Yeah, why? *(A moment.)*

BUDDY: So you *are* a virgin.

EDNA: No, I'm a trained active listener. I work the eating disorder hotline on Fridays.

BUDDY: That sounds depressing.

EDNA: You're not allowed to say depressing, unless you know what depression is. I'm allowed to say it because I'm a peer health educator.

BUDDY: I slept in your bathtub last night, I think I can use the word "depression" in a sentence. *(A slight pause.)*

EDNA: My professor . . . told me . . . we've been talking about stuff in class . . . about this idea of, um, these-Christian-fascist-ideologues-removing-the-divide-between-Church-and-State? And how that's affecting foreign policy and that's going to be really bad? Um. Are your nose hairs falling out?

BUDDY: It relaxes me.

EDNA: What — like smelling yourself?

BUDDY: Kinda. Yeah. But enough about me. What's going on with you?

EDNA: Stressed out. You know. Gearing up for midterms. Raa! And I'm a peer health educator. I'm like the best.

BUDDY: Yeah? How do you know you're the best?

EDNA: Well, the peer health educators are going into local high schools to do skits about date rape, and I got the lead. You want to help with my lines?

BUDDY: No —

EDNA: Come on. The highlighted parts are my lines. Start at the top of the page.

BUDDY: *(Reading.)* "Hey baby."

EDNA: "Hey Kevin."

BUDDY: It's "Hi Kevin."

EDNA: It doesn't matter. "Hi Kevin."

BUDDY: "There's a big party tonight at the Kappa house. There's going to be a lot of alcohol and, uh, drugs. You're going to the party, aren't you?"

EDNA: "I don't know if I should, Kevin."

BUDDY: "It's a kegger. And there will be lots of drugs."

EDNA: "Should I go?"

BUDDY: "Come on, baby, if you don't go, you're not going to be cool. And I won't go out with you anymore."

EDNA: Wait, wait — "If you're going to put those limitations —"

BUDDY: Boundaries.

EDNA: "If you're going to put those boundaries on our relationship, Kevin, then I don't think you care about, um, my belief system"?

BUDDY: Perfect.

EDNA: There's another page, there's an alternative ending where she goes to the party and gets date-raped —

BUDDY: You know that part?

EDNA: It's all like, "Stop, no, stop." We do this skit and then they decide what choice she should make — They discuss it. It's like choose-your-own-adventure.

BUDDY: I think you're going to change the life of a local high school student.

EDNA: Yeah?

BUDDY: No, this has the opposite effect, it actually makes you want to go to the party and get date-raped. I mean, *come on* — write your own. Use some imagery. Is it a big keg? What kind of beer is it? Why is his name Kevin?

EDNA: It's just — it's Kevin.

BUDDY: What if it were more evil, like Otto?

EDNA: No one is named Otto, it's not plausible.

BUDDY: Otto von Bismark, Otto Dix, Otto — Otto Heinrich Warburg —

EDNA: You're so annoying!

BUDDY: Or you could call him Fat Hands?

EDNA: My hands are proportional. Monsterface.

BUDDY: Fat hands.

EDNA: You have stupid facial hair.

BUDDY: Your knuckles are like tiny children.

EDNA: How'd you get through customs without showering? Were you wearing a hat?

BUDDY: You think you have to shower before you can reenter the country?

EDNA: I don't know — you can't bring back cheese from France.

BUDDY: Maybe they didn't know how dirty I was.

EDNA: Or maybe you were wearing a hat. Come on, get out of the tub — you're not really going to sit there, right? *(A slight pause.)*

BUDDY: You know date-rape doesn't sound so bad. Comparatively speaking.

EDNA: What do you mean? Compared to what?

END OF SCENE

The Mistakes Madeline Made
Elizabeth Meriwether

Comic
Edna, twenty-one
Wilson, late twenties

Edna suffers from Ablutophobia, the fear of bathing. Wilson is a bad poet and her casual lover.

WILSON: Tweet, tweet! *(Wilson runs in. Edna is caught with piles of handiwipes in her fists.)*
EDNA: Oh geez. Wilson.
WILSON: What are you doing?
EDNA: I don't know — I just — I think I'm taking her handiwipes and I'm holding them hostage. I think that's what I'm doing. So you can tell her or you can not — tell her — what's it going to be?
WILSON: Aaaaiii.
EDNA: What's it going to be? Are you in?
WILSON: I'm in! Ha, ha. *(Wilson laughs and grabs handfuls of wipes.)*
EDNA: I hate her.
WILSON: Me too. Meeee toooo. I hate her.
EDNA: I hate her so much.
WILSON: I hate her so so much. ChhhhhhvvvvvvvvvRING!
EDNA: What's that?
WILSON: That's how much I hate her.
EDNA: What did she do to you?
WILSON: She doesn't like my sounds.
EDNA: I like your sounds.
WILSON: You like my sounds? *(Edna nods. A moment.)*
EDNA: You want to know what the scariest thing is?
WILSON: Yes, I do want to know what the scariest thing is.
EDNA: There's a part of me that likes to file.
WILSON: Sometimes it's nice. Filing. Sometimes. Uh. Hiiii. Edna. Na. Na.

EDNA: Hi Wilson.

WILSON: Handiwipes are funny. Why? Go!

EDNA: The word. It's a funny word.

WILSON: Yes, handiwipe. Handiwipe.

EDNA: You go!

WILSON: Handiwipes are funny because, because you're carrying around a little wipe so you can wipe yourself — that's just funny, period. That's really funny.

EDNA: Who actually uses handiwipes?

WILSON: I know someone. There was a woman on a plane I sat next to. Do you have time for a story? Yeah? Okay? It's kind of interesting. So I was flying from New York to Detroit, and I like to fly because of plane sounds — Like: Fffffeeeiirr —

EDNA: Yeah —

WILSON: Yeah, okay. Whoops. Shut up Wilson. And the woman started to talk to me even though I was sitting there making sounds to myself. She was a sales rep for a stationery company — Imprintables — what are imprintables? Imprintables, imprrrrrintables. Aaah — Bing, bing, okay. She's coming back from New York where she was at a stationery conference in the Javitz Center. Boring, boring. And she didn't like to be in New York alone. And I told her that I am always alone and she told me to try internet dating.

EDNA: Did you?

WILSON: Uuuuh, no. No. I. I don't have successful blind dates.

EDNA: Okay, yeah.

WILSON: Vrrroooo. My story races ahead. So her kids asked for T-shirts — from the MTV store and from the Hard Rock Café. And she's Armenian. She liked the movie *My Big Fat Greek Wedding* and she talked about how her family was like that movie, except big, fat, and Armenian, but I didn't see that movie so then she decided to explain the plot to me in a lot of detail. This was the sound of her voice, if you took out the words: EEEEE, neeka, neeka, EEEEEE, gropop.

EDNA: Wilson, Beth is coming back soon —

WILSON: No, no, wait — her nephew was in the army fighting. And she had been a mother to him because his mother died of breast cancer when he was in high school and — snap! He doesn't graduate, joins the army, and goes over and fights and she sends him care packages but he doesn't respond. She tells him it's a waste of time and energy. He finally responds. He says hi, how are you, and then he asks her to send handiwipes. That's all he asks for. If I were in the army, I would ask for Oreos.

EDNA: Of course, me too.

WILSON: But he asks for handiwipes. And I told her. Maybe he just feels like his hands are always dirty . . . *(A slight pause.)* Do you know what I like most of all? The way a plane sounds when it lands. Very . . . complex . . . Did you enjoy my story?

EDNA: I did. A lot.

WILSON: Dong, dong, dong. *(A slight pause.)*

EDNA: What's that?

WILSON: That? That was my special bell sound . . . I've been waiting to tell that story for a long time. It kind of just sits there in my head. Do you have that? This story that just lives in your head?

EDNA: Yeah, I have that.

WILSON: Yeah?

EDNA: My brother. Lives in my head. The week he came to visit me. He's dead. He's — he is no longer with us. He is not of this earth. I don't know how to say it. I have syntax problems. He was killed a year ago.

WILSON: Hhhhooo . . . oohhh . . . Edna —

EDNA: You don't have to make your sounds. I'm fine. It's fine. *(A slight pause.)*

WILSON: Hhhooo —

EDNA: Stop. Seriously. You sound like an owl. *(A slight pause.)*

WILSON: My paper. My paper lies in my head.

EDNA: The dissertation?

WILSON: The. Big. One. I've been working on it for a long time. Long time. Ha, ha. Woo.

EDNA: What's it on?

WILSON: Leibniz. Monads.

EDNA: What?

WILSON: Leibniz's perceptual monads. The definition of the soul. Tiny bubbles of soul. *(Revving up his engine.)* Vrrrooooo . . . *(In a funny mechanical voice.)* The soul is the tiniest place that is capable of memory — the soul is any tiny space where multiple moments of time can exist at once. *(He snorts.)* NEEERRRRD.

EDNA: Wow. Tell me more.

WILSON: Okay, it's my favorite thing to talk about. *(Revving up his engine.)* Vrrrroooo . . . We have no concrete definition of memory, so there could be tiny bubbles of soul everywhere. What if there's memory in a copy machine or an old shirt . . . Or just a speck on the ground . . . so if we destroy anything, if we sweep the floor, are we killing tiny pieces of soul? How could we live that way, and also we wouldn't be able to do chores. So there has to be some things that can be thrown away or forgotten . . . And this is the problem with our power — how do we decide what to destroy? Do we forget about the copy machine? I don't want to forget about the copy machine.

EDNA: Uh-huh.

WILSON: But if we forget about the copy machine or throw out the shirt or, to get more abstract whhoooo, if we pretend like we don't know something is happening, if we forget about it, then it isn't really alive anymore . . . This is the nature of our power — just by ignoring it, we can kill it . . . Fffff! Dead . . . So what do we choose to forget? *(A moment.)* I don't know. I don't have a thesis.

EDNA: Do you have a bibliography?

WILSON: I have a working title.

EDNA: Let's hear it.

WILSON: "Tiny Bubbles of Soul." You like it?

EDNA: Yeah.

WILSON: Ming, tingy-ting!

END OF SCENE

Public Transportation
Warren C. Bowles

Dramatic
Steve, late twenties, Black
Juanita Lee, mid to late twenties, Black

Two young strangers meet on a crowded city bus.

(City bus. Steve, Black, in his late twenties, sits in a window seat reading August Wilson's 'Fences.' A backpack sits on the seat to his left. Juanita Lee, Black, mid to late twenties, boards the bus. She is dressed in a blue or green uniform or scrubs. She stands a moment looking for a seat. The bus is obviously crowded. Since there are no seats available she stands by Steve's. She notices that he neither offers her the vacant seat nor does he really seem to notice her. He reads a line then closes his eyes and mumbles the line under his breath. He is trying to learn lines.)

JUANITA LEE: Honey, you o.k.?

STEVE: Huh?

JUANITA LEE: I heard a people movin' their lips when they read but look like you really "soundin' *everything* out."

STEVE: Yeah.

JUANITA LEE: Sorry. It was a joke. *(A beat.)* Honey, you gonna let me sit down?

(She glances at the seat beside Steve and after a quick moment he notices and moves his backpack. She sits.)

(Steve smiles politely.)

JUANITA LEE: Whatcha readin'?

STEVE: This? It's a play actually. *Fences? (No response from Juanita Lee.)* By August Wilson?

JUANITA LEE: Oh? Any good?

STEVE: Uh, yeah. It's one of the greatest plays of the twentieth century, if not of all time.

JUANITA LEE: Oh. You go the U?

STEVE: No Actually I'm headed over to the South side. I'm headed over to The Mashuhuri. See, I'm not just *reading* the play I'm working on my lines. I'm understudying Gabe and Bono. *(No response from Juanita Lee.)* That's what I do. *(No response from Juanita Lee.)* I'm a professional actor.

JUANITA LEE: For real?

STEVE: Yeah.

JUANITA LEE: You sing?

STEVE: *(Sings, doing his best Luther Vandross, perhaps over doing it a bit on the final "Dove.")*

There's a Rose
In a fisted Glove
and the eagle flies
with the dove . . .

JUANITA LEE: *(He can sing:)* Hunh . . . What movies you in?

STEVE: No. I'm a local actor. On the stage. Theater.

JUANITA LEE: I been to plays. In high school they took a bunch of us to that big theater downtown.

STEVE: That's The Rep.

JUANITA LEE: They told us it was gonna be a play about some sistas. *(She laughs.)* Wasn't nothin' but White people sittin' around, talkin' in all this Shakespeare talk about how they need to get off the farm and get to Moscow or somethin'. *(She laughs again.)* I kinda liked it though. Them big cushy seats. Theater, uhn, that's some of the best sleep you can get. *(She starts digging her CD Walkman out of her bag.)*

STEVE: Oh. Well I'm working over at The Mashuhuri. *(No response from Juanita Lee.)* It's one of *the* preeminent Black theaters in the United States. Black people here are really lucky to have such a preeminent Black theater in our community. *(No response from Juanita Lee.)* It's my second time working there. Last spring I did *Holding Hands In The Park.* Marsha promised me she'd find something for me in *Fences* if I would do *Holding Hands.* So . . .

JUANITA LEE: *(Getting ready to listen to a CD but obviously surprised that she recognizes the title.)* I know about that play.

STEVE: Yeah?

JUANITA LEE: A deacon at my church was taking about it. He said it was about a couple a' faggots. Is that the one?

STEVE: Is that all he saw? But there was a lot more to the play than just that. Why do people have to reduce everything to stereotypes, that are only about what they *want* to see, not necessarily about what is actually there. How you deal with that person. An old, ignorant, backwater, bigoted . . .

JUANITA LEE: How do you know? You don't know that! You don't know Deacon Sims! *(She turns on the CD.)*

STEVE: Uh, no. You're right. I'm sorry. And I'm not trying to defend homosexuality. I mean, I'm not gay myself. Uh, obviously. There *are* gay, Black men. So there's nothing wrong with seeing them on stage. I mean, jeez, Langston Hughes, James Baldwin, uh, *(Searching. Trying to remember Roscoe Lee Brown's name:)* uh, Billy Dee Williams. *(A beat. Juanita is lost in her music.)* I mean, I'm just sensitive about the images of Black men that we do and don't see on the stage. You know what I'm saying?

JUANITA LEE: *(Singing softly:) B-A-B-Y*

STEVE: In grad school I was so thrilled when I was cast as Aaron in *Titus.*

If one good deed in all my life I did,
I do repent it from my very soul.

Even though I had to audition to even get in the program at Prairie View, 'cause now I was doing "Shakespeare" at "the big university" I thought I had arrived.

JUANITA LEE: *(Singing softly.) . . . it's like a badge of honor.*

STEVE: I was playing a White man's image of a Black man.

JUANITA LEE: *(Singing softly:) I see ya workin' ya job*
I see ya goin to school

STEVE: From the 16th century.

JUANITA LEE: *(Singing softly:) And even though ya fed up*
With makin' beds up

STEVE: "A villainous Moor, with a *fiend-like face.*" Can you believe that?

JUANITA LEE: *(Singing softly:) B-A-B-Y*

STEVE: *(He's on a roll now.)* White people always control the images. It's like The Rep. It's great they did *Top Dog* and *In The Blood* but does Suzan-Lori Parks really *need* The Public or The Rep? Is she a *great* playwright because she's produced at The Rep or does The Rep do her plays *because* she's a great playwright. Or do they think of her as just the best of the current crop of Black playwrights, you know, "the best of the rest"? How come hers are the images of Black people we need to see? You know?

Course I'd love to get that Rep salary for a while.

JUANITA LEE: *(Singing softly:) . . . in the mail.*

STEVE: And tell me. Why do they always cast out of New York? I could of played the shit out of Booth.

JUANITA LEE: *(Singing softly:) Sayin to yourself, "This here ain't fair"*

STEVE: I think I'm the only actor in town can't get cast at the fuckin' Rep.

JUANITA LEE: *(Singing softly:) What don't kill you can only make you stronger*

STEVE: I'm just glad I can sing a little. I mean, you look around nowadays there's so many theaters doing *Mahalia, Somebody Say Amen, Steal Away, Diary of a Mad Black Woman.* We're sliding back to giving the White audiences only what they want — Black folks singing and dancing and "praisin' they Jesus."

JUANITA LEE: *(Singing softly:) (She hears this last bit as she reaches across him to pull the "Stop Request" cord.) B-A-B-Y*

STEVE: Oh, you're getting off at the U. I get the uniform now. You work in housekeeping at the hospital or somewhere else on campus?

JUANITA LEE: *(Singing softly:) I know we can make it if we dream (Taking off her headphone and putting her Walkman away.)* What did you say? What did you ask me?

STEVE: The uniform. You work in housekeeping somewhere on campus?

JUANITA LEE: *(The bus stops. She is getting up to leave.)* Actually I'm a second-year Rho Chi Fellow in the Clinical and Experimental Pharmacology program. I'll tell you what, it's been real nice talking to you. Good luck to you and your preeminent little play. See ya. *(She exits.)*

END OF SCENE

Straight On Til Morning

Trish Harnetiaux

Dramatic
Peter, late twenties
Isabele, late twenties

Peter is an A&R guy (Band Scout) for a hot new record label. He oozes with charm and self-confidence, tells a great story and is the center of attention in any crowd. Isabel is Peter's best friend and a neighborhood playmate, she has always had a wicked crush on him.

(2 p.m. The bench in a park near Exxon Cafe. Isabele is sitting there waiting. She's got that waify-indie-token-chick-bass-player look. Peter enters, late.)

PETER: So listen, I can't have brunch with you.,
ISABELE: Me? I'm well, thanks for asking.
PETER: I mean it.
ISABELE: I've been waiting here for a year. It's two. Pick up your fuckin' phone.
PETER: She's pissed.
ISABELE: Leave then.
PETER: I shouldn't even be here.
ISABELE: Christ, Peter.
PETER: *(Handing her a worn copy of 'A Heartbreaking Work of Staggering Genius.')* Here's your book. God, I've been up all night —
ISABELE: *(Thrilled.)* So have I! Why do you think I'm dressed like this. It was madness — we had the most fucked up gig. Hey — where were you —
PETER: "Where were you?"
ISABELE: The show —
PETER: I totally forgot. Sorry.
ISABELE: You still haven't seen us play.
PETER: Next time, I absolutely promise.
ISABELE: That's such bullshit.

PETER: So what happened?

ISABELE: F-D-N-Y. God! It was so frustrating. We went on after this feathered little wench that sang these pansy-ass candyland vocals —

PETER: Was she hot?

ISABELE: Excuse me?

PETER: I think I know who you're talking about — headband, Indian, really cool —

ISABELE: *Um, no.* Anyway, we go on right after them, I mean people are ready to hear something real and we're halfway through the first set — it was awesome — Art had the cord of his guitar —

PETER: Listen, can we talk later? Moira's going to kill me.

ISABELE: You need to make her understand that we go back.

PETER: I know.

ISABELE: We're all gonna run into each other, small neighborhood. Stay. *(Pulls out a small flask.)* Buy ya a drink? It's your favorite liquid breakfast.

PETER: *(Whispering so no one else hears him.)* Bailey's?

ISABELE: It's your second favorite liquid breakfast.

PETER: Coffee?

ISABELE: Whiskey!

PETER: *(Taking the flask from her.)* I'm only staying for a few minutes. *(Drinks.)* Thanks.

ISABELE: She all moved in?

PETER: Yeah.

ISABELE: Playing the little lady, home making curtains for her new house?

PETER: Stop it. *(Pause.)* You'd like her.

ISABELE: I'm sure I would.

PETER: You look pretty. I like your hair.

ISABELE: I combed it.

PETER: Well, it looks nice.

ISABELE: Imagine if I washed it.

(They smile.)

PETER: So your message last night sounded pretty panicky — and kinda drunk.

ISABELE: We had the show.

PETER: Right. Where again? Lala'z?

ISABELE: Piano's.

PETER: How'd you swing that?

ISABELE: We're good.

PETER: Piano's. Cool.

ISABELE: So I didn't finish. Fire Department comes because apparently the feathered chick collapses at the bar after her set and people are basically *tripping over her* on their way to the back room where we're playing.

PETER: *(Smiling.)* Because you're so awesome.

ISABELE: Yeah dick head, because we're so awesome. So we stop playing and are all sitting there having a drink and we get in this *huge fight.*

PETER: About what?

ISABELE: The name of the band.

PETER: Holy Grail?

ISABELE: Catch up, Idol Threat.

PETER: Idle Threat?

ISABELE: I-D-L-E?

PETER: Right.

ISABELE: Right. See, that's the problem. That's how the guys thought it was spelled. It's I-D-O-L. Idol Threat.

PETER: Like Billy Idol?

ISABELE: Like American Idol.

PETER: Maybe you guys should break up.

ISABELE: No. It's *my* band.

PETER: But that's what great bands do — they break up.

ISABELE: We've only been together a couple months.

PETER: Then get back together for the reunion tour.

ISABELE: Bite me. This has to work. We're going to be on top of each other.

PETER: How'd they not know the spelling?

ISABELE: We never had to write it down. They never saw it until they saw the tour schedule. Big meeting about it all tonight.

PETER: Those are always fun.

ISABELE: *(Picking up the book.)* Did you read it?

PETER: Kinda.

ISABELE: How do you do that?

PETER: What?

ISABELE: Kinda read a book.

PETER: I skimmed it.

ISABELE: It's *the* book Peter. Instant classic.

PETER: Not really a book person.

ISABELE: The part about the Frisbee. Right on, right?

PETER: What?

ISABELE: The part where they're playing Frisbee on the beach and throw it higher and further than anyone in the history of the world has ever thrown a Frisbee before. It reminds me of us. You didn't even open it. Hello?

PETER: Price is here.

ISABELE: Price?

PETER: Uncle.

(Isabele makes noise or physical expression that means 'That's weird.')

PETER: I think it's weird too — why do you think it's weird?

ISABELE: I didn't know you had an uncle.

PETER: Right. It's freaking me out a bit. I mean, I haven't seen this guy *forever.*

ISABELE: What does he want?

PETER: I don't know.

ISABELE: Well, where is he?

PETER: Home, with Moira.

ISABELE: Right. *(Moving closer to him.)* I miss you.

PETER: Something's wrong for him to be here.

ISABELE: Are you gonna miss me? Our tour is the fucking shit. Listen to this line up — Athens, Nashville, Chapel Hill, Tampa, Silverlake, Eugene, Olympia, Austin — oh, you should meet us in Austin!

PETER: You know I can't.

ISABELE: Why not? You love Austin.

PETER: I know —

ISABELE: Get your work to send you out, research. They've done it before —

PETER: It's different now.

ISABELE: Now you're married? Jesus. *(Shivering.)* It's cold.

PETER: You should wear a coat.

ISABELE: They're too constraining.

PETER: So tell me.

ISABELE: What?

PETER: Why are we here?

ISABELE: Because you said you didn't want to eat so we're just sitting —

PETER: That's not what I mean.

ISABELE: Everyone's been saying this place is —

PETER: Isabele —

ISABELE: What —

PETER: Stop!

ISABELE: Peter — what the fuck is your problem?

PETER: Listen to yourself, you sound crazy.

ISABELE: You . . . sound crazy . . .

PETER: *(Overlapping.)* You sound crazy —

ISABELE: You sound crazy —

PETER: You sound crazy —

ISABELE: You sound crazy —

(They start laughing.)

ISABELE: Let's sneak into the pool.

PETER: I was there last night.

ISABELE: I haven't been in so long.

PETER: Don't tempt me.

ISABELE: This'll be perfect!

PETER: We'd have to bring food —

ISABELE: Stay for hours. I wonder if that fucked up mural we made is still there —

PETER: It is —

ISABELE: Let's grab some beer, call Nico, Jack —

PETER: Stop, stop, stop. I have like two minutes left in me. I have to go.

ISABELE: You're on a short leash these days.

PETER: Stop.

ISABELE: Fine. I want to ask you something.

PETER: Alright. Out with it.

ISABELE: O K.

PETER: You'll actually have to talk, use words.

ISABELE: Right.

PETER: I don't speak your fairy language.

ISABELE: Ok. You know I'm leaving tomorrow.

PETER: Yes.

ISABELE: Do you remember Rubela last month — when I was just about to leave and you were smoking a bowl with some Asian chick in that tent?

PETER: Hmmmm. Sounds like it could've happened.

ISABELE: Remember, I had to go 'cause I'd gotten sick?

PETER: Almost . . .

ISABELE: You don't remember?

PETER: Was this the night that Jack was locked on the roof all night?

ISABELE: Yeah.

PETER: Then I have no recollection.

ISABELE: Oh.

PETER: The last thing I remember was putting on some Sonic Youth CD.

ISABELE: I'd been thinking about what you said — when we were waiting for my car.

PETER: What'd I say?

ISABELE: Nothing.

PETER: Come on — was it funny?

ISABELE: No.

PETER: You know how funny I get.

ISABELE: It was sweet. You expressed your undying love for me. Told me I was the only one in the world that underst —

PETER: *(Laughing.)* That's hysterical! I didn't cry or anything, did I?

ISABELE: No, no crying.

PETER: So what about that?

ISABELE: What.

PETER: Why'd you bring it up?

ISABELE: No reason. Nothing. Honest mistake.

PETER: There's something else —

ISABELE: Kinda.

PETER: I'm not telepathic. You're acting like a girl.

ISABELE: Fuck you. Fine. So, I'm leaving tomorrow, gone forever —

PETER: Forever? Really.

ISABELE: Whatever. I just . . . I want to leave knowing exactly what your feelings for me are.

PETER: Why are you doing this —

ISABELE: I think I have a right —

PETER: God, Isabele.

ISABELE: I want to make sure I understand.

PETER: It's like you to enjoy uncomfortable situations.

ISABELE: Fuck you.

PETER: I have to go.

ISABELE: Just like that.

PETER: Just like that.

ISABELE: You're really not going to answer me?

PETER: No.

ISABELE: Vintage Peter. Vintage.

PETER: We've been over this! Have had this conversation before!

ISABELE: That was years ago!

PETER: And *nothing has changed.* Oh wait — except I moved in with my girlfriend.

ISABELE: And *that sounds fun.*

PETER: Why do you do this shit. I don't need it.

ISABELE: Peter —

PETER: — I'm sick of leaving you on corners like this. It's like you glory in being abandoned.

(Isabele slaps him hard across the face.)

ISABELE: You silly fucking ass. *(She exits.)*

END OF SCENE

Strike/Slip
Naomi Iizuka

Dramatic
Angie, teens, Asian American
Rafael, teens, Latino American

Angie and Rafael are boyfriend/girlfriend. Here, Angie tells Rafi she wants to run away somewhere.

(Late night. A rooftop in downtown Los Angeles. Traffic on a nearby freeway sparkles, an endless stream of headlights. Angie and Rafael. Rafael touches Angie's palm.)

ANGIE: *Son-ppa-lak.*
RAFAEL: *Son-ppa-lak.*
(Rafael touches Angie's face.)
ANGIE: *Ul-gool.*
RAFAEL: *Ul-gool.*
(Raphael touches Angie's eyes.)
ANGIE: *Noon.*
RAFAEL: *Noon.*
(Raphael touches Angie's mouth.)
ANGIE: *Eep.*
RAFAEL: *Eep.*
(Rafael touches Angie's lips.)
ANGIE: *Eep-sool.*
RAFAEL: *Eep-sool.*
(Rafael and Angie kiss. Angie pulls away.)
ANGIE: Why do you want to learn Korean? It's not like you're not going to remember. You're going to forget.
RAFAEL: No I'm not. *(Touching Angie's palm.) Son-ppa-lak.* See? I remember.
ANGIE: Not bad. *(Beat.)* I like this place. You feel like you're on top of the world. It's like you can see the whole city down below and it's all like twinkling. Look at all those cars. They look so tiny from

up here. Think about all those people just like in their own little worlds. Like they don't even think about what's out there. It's like they're trapped, you know. And they think that's all there is. It's like their worlds are so small and they never even wonder what else there is out there.

RAFAEL: *(Beat.)* What? What is it?

ANGIE: Nothing.

RAFAEL: No. You're like, you're like thinking about something. It's cool. Just say it.

ANGIE: Rafi, I want to go away.

RAFAEL: What do you mean?

ANGIE: I mean I want to go away.

RAFAEL: Like go where?

ANGIE: I don't know. Fiji —

RAFAEL: Fiji?

ANGIE: It doesn't matter. It doesn't matter where. Just somewhere else, anywhere else. Let's just go, Rafi, just you and me.

RAFAEL: Angie, you know I want that. You know that. I want that more than anything. After we graduate, we can take off. I promise. We can go anywhere —

ANGIE: No. Now, tonight. I want to go tonight.

RAFAEL: Tonight? Where are we gonna go tonight?

ANGIE: It doesn't matter. Somewhere else. Somewhere far away. It doesn't matter where. Rafi, please.

RAFAEL: Angie —

ANGIE: What? Say it. Just say it.

RAFAEL: Listen. Listen to me —

ANGIE: No don't.

RAFAEL: Angie —

ANGIE: No I don't want to hear it.

RAFAEL: Come on.

ANGIE: No, cause we talk about these things, we talk about all these things. And you tell me this stuff, you tell me that you love me, you tell me that we're going to have this life, that we're gonna go and have this whole life together, but you don't mean it. You don't mean any of it.

RAFAEL: That's not true. You don't know. You read your books and you go to school and you don't know how it is.

ANGIE: You asked me what I want and I'm telling you.

RAFAEL: You need money to live. You can't just go. You can't just leave with the clothes on your back. Not in real life.

ANGIE: I can get money.

RAFAEL: Where?

ANGIE: It doesn't matter.

RAFAEL: Angie —

ANGIE: What?

RAFAEL: It's not just that.

ANGIE: What then? What's stopping you?

RAFAEL: I can't just leave, Angie. I can't do that.

ANGIE: Fine. Do what you want.

(Angie starts to go.)

RAFAEL: Angie. What are you doing, where are you going, wait.

(Rafael stops her.)

RAFAEL: What's wrong with you? Did somebody do something to you? Did somebody hurt you? Who hurt you, Angie? Tell me who.

ANGIE: Why? What are you going to do about it?

RAFAEL: I will kill anyone who hurt you.

ANGIE: No, see, don't say things you don't mean. That's your problem. You're like a kid.

RAFAEL: I'm not a kid. I'm a grown man.

ANGIE: A grown man does what he says he's gonna do. A grown man doesn't talk just to hear himself talk. It's like you say things, but you don't mean them.

RAFAEL: That's not true.

ANGIE: You don't even know what I have to live with. You have no idea.

RAFAEL: Angie, please. I love you.

ANGIE: If you love me, then let's go. Let's go tonight.

RAFAEL: Angie —

ANGIE: Cause otherwise we're done. It's over. You're never gonna see me again. *(Beat.)* Yeah? Is that how it's gonna be? All right then.

(Angie starts to go.)

RAFAEL: Wait. Angie, wait. We'll go. We'll leave tonight.

ANGIE: For real?

RAFAEL: Yeah. Just go back home. Get your stuff together. I'll meet you there. It's going to be OK.

(Rafael and Angie kiss. Angie goes. Rafael remains.)

END OF SCENE

They're Just Like Us

Boo Killebrew

Dramatic
Beth, twenties to thirties
Richard, twenties to thirties

Beth and Richard broke up because he couldn't handle her obsession with acting. Richard moved away to the South to enjoy "space and roads and soft people." Beth has found Richard and broken into his new home. This scene begins after Richard has come home to find that Beth has broken in.

(Richard walks into his house. Beth is in there, pacing. He is surprised to see her.)

RICHARD: How did you get into my house?

BETH: I broke your window.

RICHARD: You broke the window?

BETH: I am a passionate person.

RICHARD: What are you going here?

BETH: I wanted to see you.

RICHARD: So you just show up and break my window?

BETH: I am an impulsive and passionate woman. Don't worry, the paparazzi don't know I'm here.

RICHARD: Okay.

(She goes to him and he pushes her away. It is awkward.)

BETH: It's really good to see you.

RICHARD: Yeah?

BETH: You know I really missed you.

RICHARD: Yeah?

BETH: Of course. It's nice to see your face.

RICHARD: Thank you.

BETH: How are you?

RICHARD: Peaceful and quiet and easy and good.

BETH: Good, are you —

RICHARD: Not a lot of buzz, buzz, buzzing going on around here, it's not loud here. I can slow down and sit still.

BETH: Yeah, I've been trying to go a little slower myself these days. I'm walking slower, leaving my cell phone at home, sitting in the park, petting dogs, calling my mom. I really have slowed down and it feels really good.

RICHARD: Yeah?

BETH: Yeah.

RICHARD: Really?

BETH: You don't believe me?

RICHARD: No, I believe you. I'm glad you're doing whatever you need to do to make yourself happy.

BETH: Thanks.

(Pause.)

RICHARD: How's the career?

BETH: Fine, I'm not really worried with it these days, like I said, I'm just trying to take it one day at a time.

RICHARD: Right.

BETH: I did get a new agent.

RICHARD: Yeah?

BETH: He really believes that I am a character actress, which is what I've known for years, so it's good that we are on the same page.

RICHARD: Great.

BETH: Oh, I did an eight-episode aarc on that show "Divine Justice."

RICHARD: Great show.

BETH: Yeah, I was the head of an Internet pedophile sex slave ring while that actor — the one who is sort of cross-eyed — talked about evidence and all that.

RICHARD: Great.

(Pause.)

BETH: I'm thinking about taking a break.

RICHARD: Really?

BETH: Yeah — just taking off and going somewhere quiet and resting and swimming and driving and all that.

RICHARD: You think you'd like that?

BETH: You know I would like that.

RICHARD: Where would you go?

BETH: Oh, I don't know. *(Gives him a little smile.)* Somewhere with space and roads and soft people.

RICHARD: Where would that be?

BETH: Why are you being an asshole?

RICHARD: What?

BETH: You know exactly how you're behaving and don't act like you don't.

RICHARD: I don't know what —

BETH: I came all the way down here! I flew down here to see you. To tell you I'm sorry! That I will stop living my life the way I was living it if that will make you happy. I want to be with you. You know that's why I'm here and you're just standing there with your one-word sentences — making me swim around in my own stupid words. You're just standing there thinking of how stupid I am.

RICHARD: I am not —

BETH: I'll do anything you want. Happily, I will give myself to you. I want to be slow and I want to be soft and I want to be with you.

RICHARD: I don't want you to change who you are, that's not what I want. I love who you are.

BETH: But you can't be with who I are!

RICHARD: I can't, but I would never want you to change for me.

BETH: What do you want? Please tell me what you want!

RICHARD: I want you to be happy.

BETH: I'm happy with you.

RICHARD: You would be for a while. Then you would start looking out again.

BETH: No, I won't. I won't look out anymore.

RICHARD: Yes, you will.

BETH: You love me, but you don't want to be with me?

RICHARD: I love you so much. I do love you.

BETH: But you don't want to be with me?

(He is quiet.)

BETH: You don't ever want to be with me?

(He doesn't answer. She cries. They are standing at opposite ends of the room.)

RICHARD: Look at all that passion.

(She looks at him.)

RICHARD: You're really good.

(She runs out.)

END OF SCENE

Victoria Martin: Math Team Queen
Kathryn Walat

Comic
Peter and Victoria, late teens

Victoria is torn between her desire to be popular and her desire to be smart. Peter is the captain of her school's math team, which she has recently joined even though it might diminish her popularity quotient, as the math team's a bunch of geeks. She is waiting for a ride home from her boyfriend, the star of the school basketball team. Here, Peter offers to take her home.

(Victoria is waiting for her ride. She looks around. Checks her watch. She's so bored she picks up The Diary of Anne Frank *and starts to read.)*

VICTORIA: "Let me put it more clearly, since no one will believe that a girl of 13 feels herself quite alone in the world. I know about 30 people whom one might call friends . . . but it's the same with all of them, just fun and joking, nothing more. I can never bring myself to talk of anything outside the common round . . . Hence, this diary." *(She flips ahead to the end of the book.)*

VICTORIA: Wait — she *dies?*

(She looks out at the audience.)

VICTORIA: She dies — *and* they read her diary?

(She chucks the book.)

VICTORIA: That is — *so* not fair.

(She pops in a piece of Big Red. Checks her watch. As she chews, she says this rhythmically to herself.)

VICTORIA: 3.141592653589793238462643383 —

PETER: Pi.

(Peter is standing right there.)

VICTORIA: Oh. You. Yeah. Pi.

PETER: I thought your ride —

VICTORIA: My ride's practice schedule must have changed. And my other ride isn't home from work yet. But they'll be here. One of them. Or, I could totally walk, I just wanted to wait until everyone else was already home, so no one would see me walking home, like I was some kind of loser who didn't have a ride.

PETER: Isn't this yours?

(He's picked up her copy of Anne Frank.*)*

VICTORIA: I believe it's Property of Longwood High School.

PETER: Look I'm — sorry about that.

VICTORIA: What?

PETER: How they told you —

VICTORIA: It wasn't you. Don't like apologize for living. It was those — those —

PETER: Gemini, Franklin and Max, that's what we call them. They've been like that since — third grade. But I let — I mean, I knew that Anne Frank wasn't conspiring with the Nazis.

VICTORIA: Right, everyone knows that. I'm so stupid.

PETER: That's not what I —

VICTORIA: You can only count on yourself.

PETER: What?

VICTORIA: You heard me, brainiac. Uno. That's what my mother says. If you want something done right — but I think she means at work, because she's pretty good at *paying* people to do things at home, like clean the house and shovel the driveway and fight with my dad about the divorce that neither of them really wants even though he's living in like California now — anyway, I should have counted on *myself.*

PETER: Your mom sounds . . .

VICTORIA: Like kind of a bitch. Yeah, thanks for clearing *that* up.

PETER: That's not what I was — forget it. Come on, I'll — give you a ride.

VICTORIA: I don't need a ride.

PETER: But I think you — do.

VICTORIA: What makes you think I want a ride *from you?*

PETER: I *think* you don't have any other choice.

VICTORIA: I could walk.

PETER: Except it's almost dark. And it's below freezing. And you're not wearing any . . . socks?

VICTORIA: *Socks* are so not cool this year.

PETER: So you'll probably be wanting this.

(He holds out Anne Frank.*)*

PETER: To pass the time, while you're sitting here, waiting for your ride.

(She looks at the book he's offering. Considers. Takes the book. Looks at its cover. Makes a face. Looks at Peter, still waiting.)

VICTORIA: I live on Glenview Road.

PETER: OK.

VICTORIA: OK.

PETER: Don't you need to get your other books?

VICTORIA: Don't you?

PETER: I already got into college. MIT. Early.

VICTORIA: I don't need my books either. I don't even need to study to pass my classes. I'm not stupid, you now. And you know something else? I am so not quitting.

Even if that's what all you nerds want me to do. You think you losers are the only one who can do math? I can do *math.* I can *do* Math Team. I'm popular, but I'm also totally, totally smart.

END OF SCENE

Victoria Martin: Math Team Queen

Kathryn Walat

Comic
Peter and Victoria, late teens

Victoria has become a member of her school's math team. Peter, the team's captain, is teaching her to drive.

(Peter's parked car. Victoria sits in the driver's seat. Peter sits next to her.)

VICTORIA: What, are you kidding? I thought I was going to *die.* Why are you — you think that's amusing? I'm serious, Peter, I almost stopped breathing and dropped *dead,* on the spot.

PETER: But you didn't.

VICTORIA: But then I was like, ew, who's gonna give me mouth-to-mouth when I pass out, so then I started breathing again. And then I . . . looked over at Jen. Sitting there sideways in her desk, pretending to be looking at the *parking lot* when really I knew she was listening to me and totally thinking: Since when does *she* do her English homework? And *then* I looked over at the other Jen, who *was* looking up at me, but I knew she wasn't listening to a word I was saying about *Catcher in the Rye.* Instead she was memorizing every inch of my outfit, so that she could pick it apart tonight on the phone.

PETER: And that made you *not* be nervous anymore?

VICTORIA: No, that made me want to be sick, but then I thought: I really don't care what they think. Or, at least for that one English class period, I cared more about Holden Caulfield. You know, Holden was a really messed up kid. Or maybe just a little lonely and confused, I don't know — that's what Max thinks. He let me practice my oral report with him. I wanted to make it really — awesome. And not just to show the Jens, or to impress Mrs. Snyder so she won't fail me in English, but like, awesome for *me.* Because that's how I want to be now.

Or, that's *who I am*, and it just took a little time for me to figure that out. But now I don't care what the Jens or anyone else at this school thinks — I'm just going to *do it.*

PETER: Do — school?

VICTORIA: Do anything! And, like, be who I am, and say how I feel — even if I feel like I'm going to —

PETER: Vomit.

VICTORIA: Yeah — actually, Peter — I'm really — sorry — about that.

PETER: Don't apologize for living, Victoria. It's not your fault I got food poisoning.

VICTORIA: I know, but you said you were sick, and I said you were just *afraid* and —

PETER: I *was* afraid.

VICTORIA: And I just wanted to *show you,* after you said that stupid thing about how with me on the Math Team there was no way in —

PETER: But that was before I even knew —

VICTORIA: But you *said* it, and that means you must have thought it. And when Jimmy said that you had said that, I — felt this pit in my stomach because I hated the way that sounded.

And I hated most of all knowing that if I were you, I probably would have thought that about me too. So when we actually made it to States, I knew that I needed to *do this,* to *show you* that —

PETER: You didn't need to show me anything.

VICTORIA: Whatever, Peter, what does that even *mean* —

PETER: I was being an idiot —

VICTORIA: Especially since you've been acting all weird every since —

PETER: Every time you were near, I felt weird, like I might —

VICTORIA: OK, I'm sorry I make you feel like *vomiting.*

PETER: No, it's not like —

VICTORIA: You didn't call me back.

PETER: What?

VICTORIA: You never called me back.

PETER: But you're the one who didn't call *me* back —

VICTORIA: But then I did!

PETER: During the student council meeting, when you *knew* I wouldn't be able to —

VICTORIA: How am I supposed to know when stupid student council meets —
PETER: Every Tuesday night.
VICTORIA: I'm not like the senior class Treasurer!
PETER: You've been at this school for *two years.*
VICTORIA: OK, student council is *not* as cool as you might think, Peter.
PETER: I wasn't going to call you back when I thought you clearly didn't even want to talk to me.
VICTORIA: OK, *that* is really — flawed reasoning. And totally *not clear.* And by the way, I really don't need to practice driving your car around this parking lot, so maybe I should just walk home.
PETER: You're walking home?
VICTORIA: I said *maybe.* God, aren't you even listening to me?
PETER: But I thought we were going to have a driving lesson.
VICTORIA: Actually, my mom's been letting me drive. On real roads. Actually, I drove on the highway last week. So clearly I *don't* need to be sitting here.
PETER: So then why did you say *yes* when I asked if you wanted to practice driving my car around the school parking lot?
VICTORIA: Peter, are you *really* such an idiot?
(They sit there. She makes a move to leave.)
PETER: Victoria, will you go to the prom with me?
VICTORIA: What?!
PETER: Does that mean yes?
VICTORIA: It means — like — I thought you didn't care about any of that *normal* high school stuff?
PETER: I thought I didn't either, but now I think — maybe I do. I don't know anymore. It's like an alien sucked out my brain, and I hardly know how to tie my sneakers, and it's not even the prom, it's more just like — me thinking about you.
VICTORIA: And did you ever think I might need time to get a dress? The prom is in like three days!
PETER: The only thing I know is, I want to be with you, Victoria. Like, all the time. Or, like even for five seconds. Because, five seconds with you — in the hallway or across the cafeteria, trying to get behind you in the hot-lunch line even when I'm not getting hot lunch, or trying to see you before you walk into Spanish when I'm on my way to calculus —

VICTORIA: Second period Thursday.

PETER: And when I look over at you, and you're looking at me, and I think maybe you're thinking what I might be thinking it's like —

VICTORIA: Two brains, both thinking the same thing.

(He says with difficulty.)

PETER: 3.1415926535897932384626. That's — all I know now. And I know it's only the first 24 decimal places, but — wait, how many do you know?

VICTORIA: 52.

PETER: That's — amazing. Victoria Martin, you *amaze* me.

VICTORIA: But I would like you even if you only knew a quarter of that.

PETER: Just six digits?

VICTORIA: Or three.

PETER: 3.14. But everyone knows —

VICTORIA: But it's — different. When you say it, it's like . . .

(Victoria kisses Peter. It's sweet.)

VICTORIA: *Pi.*

PETER: Pi.

(They kiss some more.)

END OF SCENE

Scenes for Two Men

All This Intimacy
Rajiv Joseph

Comic
Seth and Ty, twenties

Seth is Ty's best buddy. Ty is a published poet who teaches at a college. Ty has quite a problem: he has gotten not one but three women pregnant!

NO JOKE

(Ty and Seth in Ty's apartment.)
SETH: Please tell me this is a joke.
TY: It's not.
SETH: You're shitting me. I know you. You're shitting me.
TY: Seth, I'm telling you.
SETH: Okay!
Okay, *Jen.*
And the neighbor? That neighbor you were . . . ? You were . . . ?
TY: Yes. Maureen.
SETH: How *old* is she?
TY: She's forty-two.
SETH: Forty-two? She's *forty-two* years old?
TY: Yes, okay?
SETH: No, Ty, this is not happening. One girl. One girl. Jen.
TY: *Three,* Seth. *Three.*
SETH: No.
TY: Yes.
SETH: Jesus.
TY: I know.
SETH: Fuck!
TY: That's what I'm saying!
SETH: I don't understand. How can this happen?
TY: I don't know. I don't know!

SETH: This is messed up!
TY: What am I going to do?
SETH: And who else? You said three! Who's the third? Who's the third girl?
TY: You don't know her.
SETH: Well who is she?
TY: Why does it matter? I am in serious shit.
SETH: Some random girl? Who? Ty, who is it?
TY: I need you to not freak out on me.
SETH: Who's the third girl? Who's the third fucking girl?!

(Beat.)

TY: She's this . . . She's a girl from work.
SETH: Your *student!?*
TY: Seth . . .
SETH: Your *student?!* Ty, your *student?!*
TY: Just calm down.
SETH: How old?
TY: Seth . . .
SETH: How old?

(Beat.)

TY: Eighteen.

(Seth freaks.)

TY: Stop it.
SETH: *Eighteen! Forty-two! Thirty!*
TY: Jen's 28.
SETH: Whatever!
TY: Listen, Seth . . .
SETH: Wait! Can you please just . . . tell me! You had sex with three different women in one week!?
TY: It wasn't all the same week, it was like over a nine-day period.
SETH: That's dirty. That's extremely dirty.
TY: It just . . . happened.
SETH: What were you thinking?! Can you tell me that? What were you thinking?
SETH: How does a condom not work?
TY: How does it *ever* work is a better question. I mean they're made of LATEX. Shouldn't it rip? We rub it and roll it and pinch it and squeeze it and slap it around and it's still supposed to protect us!?

SETH: This is a huge mess.

TY: And it's supposed to be *thin.* Thin, so we can feel *through* it. So we can pretend it's not there.

SETH: I came over here, and I thought, *Jen is pregnant. This is a big mess.* But now you drop the other two on me, and I swear to God, Ty, you are so fucked. You are so so so fucked.

TY: I know.

SETH: I'm not going to lie to you.

TY: Thanks.

SETH: Look: Are you 100 percent certain with each one?

TY: What do you mean?

SETH: A: Do the other girls know for sure they're pregnant? And B: Are you absolutely certain you are the father?

TY: I'm pretty sure.

SETH: Well, "pretty sure" is not 100 percent.

TY: I'm pretty sure! I'm sure! I'm 100 percent sure.

SETH: Let me tell you something, man. Franny? Franny is out of her mind.

TY: I know . . .

SETH: She is frothing at the mouth. She will have your head, man. And guess who's getting the brunt of it every moment of every day?

TY: You are.

SETH: I am! I am getting raked over the coals because you knocked up her big sister and she is one pissed-off bride-to-be right now!

TY: What do you want me to say? Franny's pissed off? *Your* problem. Your problem is a lot smaller than my *problems.* Franny's annoying you? Guess what Seth? News Flash! Franny is an annoying little cooze! She was born that way! And I say this with all due respect, no offense.

SETH: None taken.

TY: Good. So I could care less as to how mad Franny is, okay? She wants my head, tell her to come and fucking take it. I don't use it anyway.

SETH: I'm just telling you, this is not small potatoes.

TY: Small what?

SETH: Potatoes.

TY: What?

SETH: Forget it. Look, with those other girls? That's your business, deal with them however you want. But I am connected to Jen, okay? She's going to be my sister-in-law.

TY: And I'm your best friend. Who's more important, Seth? Your future sister-in-law or your best friend since the first grade?

SETH: My future wife.

TY: Oh, you are a pussy. Oh my god, you are such a pussy.

SETH: All I'm saying is please do *something.*

TY: Like what?

SETH: Apologize! Start with that! Jen is freaked out, do you get that!? She tells you she's pregnant and you go crazy on her!? I mean the way she explains it, it was like she had turned into some giant mutant worm.

TY: I was freaking out!

SETH: It doesn't matter! She's a mess.

TY: So I apologize? Then what? What do I say? Jen, sweetheart, you should know you're not alone, I knocked up a couple more chicks while I was at it.

SETH: Tell her *something.*

TY: What? What do I say? How do I explain this?

SETH: I don't know.

I don't know!

(Beat.)

I DON'T KNOW!

END OF SCENE

Asylum

Keith Aisner

Comic
Gary, twenties
God, ageless

While he is dreaming Gary conjures up God. Gary hopes that when God explains what kind of a person Gary is, He'll reveal what it takes to be completely happy.

GOD: So, did you want to talk to me about something, or . . .?

GARY: Yeah, I did. I'm not an unhappy person, but I'd like to somehow make it easier to be happier. So I've been having symbolically powerful beings such as yourself work their juju on me, but when I wake up, nothing's changed. When that didn't work I asked these gods to tell me what will make me happy, and they gave me answers you'd expect to find in greeting cards. So . . . what I'd like you to do is explain me. You be the pipeline into my psyche. Tell me why I act the way I do. Tell me where I fit in the scope of things . . . all of it. Drill as deep as you need to go.

GOD: And by knowing yourself you'll discover happiness?

GARY: Right.

GOD: You're sure that's your goal?

GARY: Yep.

GOD: Finding happiness through self-understanding.

GARY: Absolutely.

GOD: 'Cause that's not such a simple . . .

GARY: I'm very prepared. I've been preparing . . .

GOD: You may not want to hear why you're not happy . . .

GARY: I am open to whatever . . .

GOD: . . . you're a bad person.

GARY: I'm . . . what?

GOD: You're a sinner.

GARY: I'm a sinner?

GOD: Yes. And that is why you're not happy.

GARY: Wait, wait, wait . . . now . . . you're just . . . I mean . . . I'm . . . I'm not a Christian.

GOD: You don't have to be a Christian to sin.

GARY: Well, you . . . but . . . okay, then define sin.

GOD: Sin is selfishness. When you put your desires above the interests of others you defy goodness.

GARY: See, I didn't know this. Selfishness is sin? Did I not get the memo? I mean, it's not a commandment . . . is it?

GOD: Gary, read between the lines. Every commandment is about putting my needs above your own. And besides, everyone knows when they're being selfish because being selfish makes you feel guilty. So you have no excuse.

GARY: What about psychotics? Sociopaths don't feel guilty.

GOD: We're talking about you, Gary. Are you a sociopath?

GARY: Well, it's never too late to start. Shit. So I'm selfish more than I'm giving?

GOD: By a long shot.

GARY: No. Bullshit.

GOD: I told you you wouldn't want to hear this.

GARY: But I do selfless things, good things, all the time.

GOD: What good things?

GARY: Oh, come on!

GOD: Seriously. What good things, Gary?

GARY: Well . . . right off the top of my head . . . when I was fourteen I spent most of my summer restoring a playground in a poor neighborhood. Alright? I volunteered and I was fourteen, which is a very selfish age.

GOD: You volunteered only after you found out Jenny Fisher would be there helping out, too. And then, when she showed no interest in you, you quit. After that you lied to your buddies and told them you'd had sex with her.

GARY: But . . . I've done a lot of good things.

GOD: Such as . . . ?

GARY: Such as when I would read to old people at convalescent homes.

GOD: You secretly hoped that you might charm one of them into leaving you something when they died.

GARY: That wasn't the main reason!

GOD: But it was a reason. Remember Mrs. Cardena? You chose to spend more time with her rather than Mr. Miller because she wore jewelry that looked expensive.

GARY: *And* because Mr. Miller smelled like rancid milk!

GOD: Which you no doubt would have tolerated had you known he was wealthy and had no children.

GARY: Well. Shit. What about . . . ?

GOD: Nope.

GARY: What about . . . ?

GOD: . . . Don't embarrass yourself.

GARY: But . . . as a general rule, I am nice to people.

GOD: You're only nice to people because you like to interpret whatever approval others may show you as proof that you're not a bad person.

GARY: That is not true!

GOD: Then why do people hurt your feelings? If you truly knew you were a good person it wouldn't matter what anyone thought of you.

GARY: I think I'm getting a migraine.

GOD: Hey, tip of the iceberg. We haven't even touched on your masturbation fantasies yet.

GARY: No!

(Pause.)

There's gotta be some kind of catch here.

GOD: No catch, Gary. You're simply a bad person.

GARY: Why? Why am I bad?

GOD: Because I said so. I'm God.

END OF SCENE

County Line

Christina Hamm

Dramatic
Caleb & Walden, seventeen

Caleb, the most popular boy in his high school, renounces his friends and social status to befriend a strange, out-of-this-world new kid in school named Walden. Caleb learns for the first time in his life what it means to be an outsider and Walden learns what it's like to be human.

CALEB: I'm sorry. I tried to warn you.
WALDEN: It's okay. They're obviously no reflection of who you are.
CALEB: They used to be.
(Caleb throws his homecoming crown into the bushes.)
WALDEN: Don't.
(Walden goes to retrieve it.)
CALEB: You keep it. I don't want any reminders of them laughing behind my back.
WALDEN: What do you have to do to get one of these?
CALEB: Be popular.
WALDEN: That's all?
CALEB: You make it sound easy.
WALDEN: Isn't it?
CALEB: Not when you have about fifteen hundred students who hate your guts.
WALDEN: Well, you look like you don't let the pressure get to you.
CALEB: Maybe because I "dance" on the inside.
WALDEN: How do you do that?
CALEB: That's called a joke. Sorta.
WALDEN: I wanna learn.
CALEB: What? How to dance?
WALDEN: How to be like you — popular.
CALEB: It's not something you learn — you gotta earn it.

WALDEN: How?

CALEB: By inflicting cruel and unusual punishment on others.

WALDEN: They took most of my powers before I came here, but I could come up with something.

CALEB: You have to have a strong constitution. You can't buckle under peer pressure or suddenly get a conscience.

WALDEN: Aliens — we don't have a conscience.

CALEB: How can I be more like you?

WALDEN: You can let me separate your soul from the rest of your body.

CALEB: Really?

WALDEN: Uh, no. You've seen too many episodes of "The X-Files."

CALEB: Oh.

WALDEN: I ran into Zoe at Xerious Records. Did she tell you guys?

CALEB: No.

WALDEN: She spoke to me — first.

CALEB: Really?

WALDEN: She was with some guy. He was wearing a Southfolk High varsity jacket.

CALEB: Southfolk? That's the other side of town. When the hell did she start hanging out with kids from another high school?

WALDEN: I don't know. But, they seemed — close.

CALEB: I've known Zoe a long time but sometimes she can be distant.

WALDEN: It seems to me that's the only thing human beings do really well — long distance.

CALEB: Reina — what was that all about?

WALDEN: She's not ready. That's all.

CALEB: God, this is hard. They're the only friends I've had. We've never really been apart.

WALDEN: You've never had any other friends?

CALEB: We did, but Bobby moved to Arizona when his dad's company transferred him — sophomore year. Looking back on it — it was the best thing for him.

WALDEN: And, he was human?

CALEB: Well . . . yeah. Sorta.

WALDEN: But, here you are hanging out with me because you want to. That means a lot.

CALEB: Same here.

WALDEN: Free will's something that can never be taken away from you. Believe me — we've tried.

CALEB: My dad's always trying to break me down. Make a man outta me — so he says.

WALDEN: Parents . . . they wanna help. Most times they mean well.

CALEB: Last time my dad meant well he got tickets for us to go to a Twins-White Sox game. I was six.

WALDEN: I must tell you something.

CALEB: What?

WALDEN: Back on the highway — my parents — they brain sanded you.

CALEB: So, you lied to me?

WALDEN: To protect you.

CALEB: You really do know what it's like to be human, don't you?

END OF SCENE

Dark Play; Or, Stories For Boys

Carlos Murillo

Seriocomic
Adam and Nick, teens

Adam and Nick are two friends who have met on the internet. What Adam doesn't know is that Nick is manipulating him.

ADAM: Your mom's pretty cool.
NICK: No she's not.
ADAM: I think she's cool.
NICK: That's cause she was hitting on you.
ADAM: She was not.
NICK: You don't know my Mom.
Your coming is like
The first time she's been that close to a man in
ADAM: What about your step dad?
NICK: My *step dad's* got plenty of other places to dunk his you know what.
ADAM: And she was hitting on me?
NICK: Dude, what are you blind or something?
ADAM: Your mom is kinda hot.
NICK: Dude. That's my mom you're talking about.
ADAM: Sorry, I was just
Kidding.
Hey, where's Rachel's room?
NICK: Upstairs. Second floor.
ADAM: Can we like
You know
NICK: You wanna check out my sister's room?
ADAM: Well,
Yeah,
I mean

NICK: What are you a stalker?

ADAM: No,

I just thought

NICK: What do you think she'd do if she found out?

ADAM: Forget it, man

NICK: "Hey Sis, guess what, you know that guy you've been mooning about? The one you met on the internet?"

ADAM: Forget it, Nick.

NICK: "Yeah, well he came over and you know what he wanted to do?"

ADAM: Nick.

NICK: "He wanted me to sneak him into your room."

ADAM: Shut up.

NICK: "So he could sniff around your panty drawer."

Hey.

Don't push.

ADAM: Just shut the fuck up, all right?

NICK: I was just kidding

ADAM: Look. This totally sucks. I'm gonna go.

NICK: NO

I mean

You can go if you want to

But.

I wanna show you something.

ADAM: What?

NICK: I took him over to a file cabinet in the basement storage area.

ADAM: This better be good.

NICK: I opened the bottom drawer

reached towards the back

pulled out a thin folder.

I sat next to Adam on the floor,

And looked him sharp in the eye.

What's my name?

ADAM: Uhhh . . . Nick?

NICK: What's my *full* name?

ADAM: This is stupid.

NICK: Come on, what's my full name?

ADAM: Your full name is Nick Suttcliffe.
NICK: Right. Nick Suttcliffe.
What does it say at the top here?
ADAM: "Birth Certificate."
NICK: And what does it say here?
ADAM: "Nick . . ."
Wait a minute.
NICK: Creepy, isn't it.
ADAM: That's not your last name.
NICK: That *is* my name.
Only no one —
Except my mom and me —
And now you —
Knows it.
ADAM: How do you know it isn't somebody else's?
NICK: How old am I Adam?
ADAM: Fourteen?
NICK: And what does it say here.
ADAM: Date of birth // November 30, 1988
NICK: November 30, 1988.
My birthday, Adam.
ADAM: Dude that's fucked up.
Wait.
Isn't that today?
NICK: Yep.
ADAM: Oh.
NICK: I'm fifteen today.
ADAM: Oh.
NICK: I was fourteen yesterday.
But I'm fifteen today.
ADAM: Oh
Well
Happy uhh
birthday
NICK: Thanks.
ADAM: Wait:
Did you ever ask your Mom about this?

NICK: No fucking way.
ADAM: But don't you wanna know?
NICK: Sure I wanna know.
I don't go a single night,
Where I don't toss and turn in my bed
Wondering
Who's my real Dad?
See:
Until I found this
My Mother?
That psycho upstairs?
Led me to believe that her "first" husband was my dad.
And when he shot himself
ADAM: He shot himself?
NICK: When I was eleven.
He disappeared one night.
Cops found him the next morning
In his car
In the parking lot of a Jewel Osco
Sucking on the wrong end of a rifle barrel.
ADAM: Holy shit.
Wait:
What's a Jewel Osco.
NICK: Supermarket chain.
Back in Chicago.
They don't have them here.
ADAM: Nick — that's
Whoa.
NICK: It wasn't until we were packing up the house there
That I found this.
Realized
My whole fucking life was a lie.
The dead guy in the parking lot —
The guy who I thought was my father —
He wasn't my father.
He was just
Some guy.

ADAM: Dude . . .
If that happened to me,
Man I'd go straight to my Mom
Shove this right in her face and be like
"What the fuck?!?!"

NICK: Oh I've been tempted.
But
I'm holding onto this little secret
In case I ever need to go nuclear on her

ADAM: Whoa.

NICK: A beautiful silence hung in the room.
A silence filled with awe. With mystery.
Intoxicating.
Adam looked
Beautiful

END OF SCENE

Dog Sees God: Confessions of a Teenaged Blockhead

Bert V. Royal

Comic
Van and CB, teens

This play imagines what the characters from "Peanuts" might be like as teenagers. Here, Van and CB (guess who?) are sharing a joint.

(CB and Van sit on the sad remnant of a brick wall. Van is smoking a joint. He offers it to CB.)

VAN: You wanna hit this?

CB: No. thanks.

VAN: *(Smiling.)* It's kind bud. You sure, man?

CB: Nah, I'm good.

VAN: I've been meaning to tell you — I'm sorry about your dog.

CB: Thanks, man.

VAN: He was a good dog.

CB: Yeah. He was.

VAN: But he was old. It was long past his time. Still — he was a good dog. I totally wanted to come to your funeral party thingy, but I was waiting on a delivery from the Doober.

CB: What do you think happens when we die?

VAN: Do you mean, like, do I believe in heaven?

CB: Yeah.

VAN: Nah, man. I'm a Buddhist.

CB: Since when?

VAN: It's kind of a new development.

CB: Well, what do Buddhists believe happens when you die?

VAN: Buddha believed that one of two things happens. Either you are reborn or you dissolve into nothingness. Oddly enough, the former is punishment and the latter, reward. We Buddhists believe that the corporeal body is the source of all suffering and a liberation from the body into nothingness, or nirvana, is the fuckin' way to go.

CB: Don't you find that depressing?

VAN: Liberation?

CB: Nothingness.

VAN: I think I'd kind of like to be nothingness. Because even nothing is something, right? *(He shows his hand to CB.)* What am I holding in my hand?

CB: Nothing.

VAN: One would say that, yes. But in that nothingness is a thousand things, right? Particles and atoms and tens of thousands of things that we might not even know about yet. I could be holding in my hand the secrets of the universe and the answers to everything.

CB: You're stoned.

VAN: Damn straight. *(CB laughs.)* Why this interest in the afterlife? Is this about your dog?

CB: Just curious.

VAN: Dude, we all have to let go of things from our childhood. Do you remember when you and my sister burned my blanket to teach me that?

CB: Yeah. It was only two months ago. If I'd known that it would lead to her being — well — I wouldn't have let her do it.

VAN: I was so pissed at you guys.

CB: The thing was fuckin' nasty, man.

VAN: *(Pissed.)* Still. Y'all suck.

CB: I think you were about to make a point.

VAN: I was?

CB: Never mind. I think I got it.

VAN: My point is, Chuck B., that life — it does go on. Even without the things that have been there since the beginning. The things that we think define us, don't mean shit in the grand scheme of things. Us defines us. Not things or other people or pets. Like, me without my blanket — it's still me. I miss my fuckin' blanket, though. That was a dick thing y'all did.

CB: Three words for you, bro — *(One finger.)* Pubic. *(Two fingers.)* Lice. *(Three fingers.)* Infestation.

VAN: Could've been fixed.

CB: Hey, we let you keep the ashes.

VAN: I smoked 'em.

CB: You what?

VAN: I rolled 'em with some good herb and smoked that shit up.

CB: That's sick.

VAN: Now, my blanket and I are like one forever.

CB: That's seriously disturbed, dawg.

VAN: We all handle grief in different ways.

CB: Can't be good for you.

VAN: Dude! Showed you two! Tryin' to mess with my shit. HA!

CB: Hey, how is your sister doing?

VAN: She's good. The doctors say that she's getting better. *(Beat.)* Damn, I miss that bitch.

CB: So do I.

VAN: This conversation is a major downer, amigo. Dead dogs, burning blankets. Let's talk about something happy.

(They sit in silence. The lights fade slowly out.)

END OF SCENE

Dues
Dwight Hobbes

Dramatic
Jorge, Kevin, thirties

Jorge is an editor of a newspaper and Kevin is his theatre critic. Jorge tells Kevin that he is in hot water about a recent review he wrote.

(The Gazette, a daily newspaper. End of the day. Jorge is at his desk sleeves rolled, looking over a contract. Phone rings. He looks at the screen on the telephone. Lifts receiver.)

JORGE: Hi, Izma . . . Kevin here?
(Reflects.)
Send him in.
(Knock on door.)
It's open.

KEVIN: *(Entering:)* Jorge, yo'.

JORGE: What's up?

KEVIN: Y' said come see you. I'm here.

JORGE: Yeah, so you are. Have a seat.
(Kevin sits.)
Here it is, sweet and plain. Good luck on your next assignment, wherever it is. 'Cause it won't be here.

KEVIN: . . . Get out.

JORGE: I shit thee not.

KEVIN: Why?

JORGE: 'Cause you messed up is why.

KEVIN: Don't tell me. The suits are on your case again about me being outspoken.

JORGE: Bah. They been on me about you since I gave you the beat. Hell, they handed me my head when I suggested putting you on staff. It's beyond that, now.

KEVIN: Man, what did I do?

JORGE: The review of that play at The Theatre Institute.

KEVIN: What? I nailed 'em dead to rights. How they gon' do *To Kill a Mockingbird* and call that lynched nigger a tribute to Black History Month? It's a typical example just what I said it was. How'd I put it? Oh, yeah. "another lily-white, luxury venue pretending to pay respect, raking in that multi-culti funding dollar." I backed every word.

JORGE: That's not the — .

KEVIN: The hell you mean, that's not the point?

JORGE: Mi amigo. You wanna take some of that bass out of voice?

KEVIN: *(Modifies his tone:)* . . . How iss not the point?

JORGE: As many enemies as you've apparently gone out of your way to make, you ask me a question dumb as that. The name Vanessa Watkins ring a bell?

KEVIN: Sure. She was in *Mockingbird*. Couldn't act wet if she fell in a lake. And that's pretty much how I put it in the review. Backed that up, too. So?

JORGE: So, you had dealings with her before I gave you the assignment, yes?

KEVIN: We both ushered at the Downtown Theatre Group. She ain't there anymore. I repeat: so?

JORGE: I'll give you "so" you dimwit. While she was there, she made a complaint and the supervisor called you on the carpet, right?

KEVIN: Yeah.

JORGE: Well, Watkins is claiming your comments about her acting actually are payback for that incident.

KEVIN: She's full of —

JORGE: Why didn't you tell me one of the actors you'd be critiquing had accused you of sexual harassment?

KEVIN: 'Cause, man, there wasn't nothing to it. She's a nutjob who just has to get attention. In fact, she just lost an acting job for that very thing. Harassing the artistic director over at, uh, whatchacallit. Ringin' the man at home, tryin' to slide up on him in rehearsal. Ask anybody over there.

JORGE: None of that has to do with anything. If you harassed her or not, if she's crazy or not. There was a conflict of interest. Which you should've told me about.

KEVIN: Conflict of interest, my b'hine. I didn't pan her because she filed a false complaint. I panned her because she can't act worth a damn. Hell, Pat Shore was in the same show. I wouldn't piss on her to put out a fire, but she did a fine job. And I said so. I'm enough of a pro not to let personal pettiness decide what I write.

JORGE: Yeah, sure: I can see the little halo. Look, I don't care what you said about Pat Shore. Watkins is the one who ran crying to the St. Paul Theatre Institute artistic director. According to him, literally in tears. Added to which, Don Whatshisface has never particularly liked you.

KEVIN: What he doesn't like is the fact that I call him on his pretentious, lily-white bullshit.

JORGE: You should have excused yourself from the assignment.

KEVIN: Wait. I'm supposed to miss a paycheck because she's a moron?

JORGE: I don't get where you get off at calling anybody a moron. You didn't even give me a heads-up. No indication at all that there might be some static — from one of the most influential producers in town. Mm-mn, my man, you don't get to call anyone "moron." 'Cause, you got that paycheck alright. But you won't be getting anymore from The Gazette.

KEVIN: Come on. You're gonna be a uptight asshole —

JORGE: What'd I just tell you about name calling?

KEVIN: You gon' let him tell you how to do your job.

JORGE: Hey, this time it's out of my hands. Not even my decision to make, homes. Shit, I might be walking out the door right along with you. If they weren't afraid to fire two minorities at once. None of the people I answer to liked the idea of my giving you the beat in the first place. I don't think I've really had a minute's peace this past year without hearing from somebody you pissed off. Now, you've finally given a lot of people who can't stand your guts — both here at the paper and all over the rest of town — a big reason to smile.

KEVIN: Don't you think your bosses are overreacting? I mean, they could just suspend me.

JORGE: I know they're overreacting. For that matter, they know they're overreacting. And don't give a shit. Because they finally got rid of you on grounds where, for once, you can't go shootin' your mouth off about racism.

KEVIN: Fuck.

JORGE: Yeah, in a nutshell. Can I tell you what pisses me off?

KEVIN: What pisses you off?

JORGE: You fucking knew better. I know you knew better, because you're not totally stupid. Just dumb enough to go ahead and do it anyway. The more you stick your neck out the better you have to cover your ass. It's just basic common sense.

(Unlocks desk drawer. Takes out bottle of Jack Daniels.)

Ah, what's done is done.

(Gestures toward shelf.)

KEVIN: *(Gets mugs from shelf.)* Easy for you to say.

JORGE: Yo', my good man, don't bitch up on me.

(Pours.)

This just could teach you a good lesson the hard way: you can't afford to make but so many mistakes. And no dumb ones.

(Raising mug.)

Salud.

JORGE: You do see and accept that you fucked up? 'Cause, actually, I haven't heard you cop to it. So, — ?

KEVIN: Yes. I fucked up. Mud n' yer eye.

JORGE: See? You're a man of honor and integrity. Now, sign this, finish your drink and then get out of my office. I wanna go home and chase my wife around the couch.

KEVIN: What's this, a contract?

JORGE: Very good.

KEVIN: To do a lead feature.

JORGE: It's dated last week. Anyone asks, this was already in the works.

KEVIN: Cool, man, thanks. Uh . . . a lead feature on what?

JORGE: You'll think of something.

KEVIN: Oh, shit. You're giving me my back to just do my thing.

JORGE: No holds barred.

KEVIN: Way to hook me up.

JORGE: Yeah, right. Listen, there's this guy, one of those holdover hippies, starting up a counter culture weekly. You'd be a perfect fit as the "angry black columnist."

KEVIN: Long as the check don't bounce.

JORGE: *(Scribbles on a note pad.)* Here's the guy's name and phone number. I spoke to him. You want the gig, it's yours. Pays chicken feed, but it is regular.

KEVIN: Fine by me.

JORGE: Now, please, do yourself a favor. Me, too, since I'm recommending you. Don't fuck up.

KEVIN: Cross my heart and hope to eat a dead frog.

JORGE: Good. Well, don't let the door hit you in the ass.

KEVIN: Okay, I'm gone.

(They shake hands. Quick hug. He exits.)

JORGE: *(Looks at proofs on his desk.)* Mañana. *(On phone:)* Izma, mira. We will deal with the proofs in the morning. And, we're holding lead space. End of the month. Listen, do you need a ride home, 'cause it wouldn't be a problem at all. Okay. G'night.

(Puts bottle back. Rolls his sleeve down, puts jacket on. Calls her back:)

Isma, I didn't mean anything by that, okay?

Never mind. See you tomorrow.

(Exits.)

END OF SCENE

Indian Blood

A. R. Gurney

Seriocomic
Eddie and Lambert, teens

Lambert is Eddie's cousin and arch-nemesis. Eddie is in trouble for having circulated a pornographic drawing. He thinks it has been destroyed but it turns out Lambert has a copy.

LAMBERT: You could at least be polite and say hello, Eddie.

EDDIE: Oh right. *(Giving Lambert the Indian sign.)* How.

LAMBERT: How what?

EDDIE: "How" happens to be a greeting between Indians, Lambert. As you damn well know.

LAMBERT: I was still thinking about Dickens.

EDDIE: Oh really? *(To audience.)* See what a twerp he is? *(To Lambert.)* Maybe you should do some thinking about how you tried to mess me up with my own grandmother.

LAMBERT: By doing what?

EDDIE: Telling her what happened at school, that's what. Thanks a bunch, pal.

LAMBERT: I just said . . .

EDDIE: I know what you just said. But it didn't work. I'm back in her good graces.

LAMBERT: For now, at least.

(Sounds of party, muted, offstage.)

EDDIE: What do you mean by that, Lambert?

LAMBERT: Come into the lavatory. I'll show you something.

EDDIE: What've you got?

LAMBERT: That's for me to know, and you to find out.

(He moves to a lighted area downstage. Eddie follows.)

EDDIE: So?

LAMBERT: *(As if locking the door.)* Hold your water. Just hold your water. *(Reaches into a pocket, produces a folded piece of paper.)* How about this? *(He unfolds it.)* Take a gander.

EDDIE: Oh Jeez! *(To audience.)* It's that same damn lousy drawing I did over at the Garver's . . . *(To Lambert.)* Ted said he'd put it in the incinerator!

LAMBERT: He forgot to light it.

EDDIE: Which means you stole it. Which means once again that the Tuscaroras are a bunch of thieving rascals and scamps.

LAMBERT: Knock it off!

EDDIE: *(Making a grab for it.)* Then give it back.

LAMBERT: *(Holding it away from him.)* No . . .

EDDIE: May I have my own personal property back, please, Lambert.

LAMBERT: No.

EDDIE: I'll give you five dollars for it. *(Takes it out of his pocket, displays it.)* Five whole dollars. Which I'll bet you can use, too, because you don't have much money. *(To audience.)* And which is a lot of money to spend on a minor work of art.

LAMBERT: This is a valuable masterpiece, Eddie. I'll take twenty.

EDDIE: Twenty *dollars?*

LAMBERT: Two-zero.

EDDIE: You bastard! You know I don't have that much.

(Eddie makes a grab for the drawing. He and Lambert get into another fight.)

(Harvey comes in.)

HARVEY: Boys? *(Looks around, then knocks on the lavatory door.)* Boys! What's going on in there?

LAMBERT: *(Now in Eddie's hammerlock.)* Eddie spilled something on his pants and I'm helping him clean up.

EDDIE: *(To audience.)* See what a natural liar he is!

HARVEY: Well make it snappy, you two, because we're about to go in to dinner. *(He goes off.)*

EDDIE: OK, Lambert. If you show that around to anyone, I'll just say I didn't draw it. Sometimes you have to lie just to keep the ball rolling.

LAMBERT: *(Looking at drawing.)* Yeah well, I notice your name on this, Eddie! I see your own personal signature.

EDDIE: Oh shit! *(To audience.)* This is what I get for being too conceited and putting my name on a crummy work of art . . . *(To Lambert.)* Lambert, my friend, let me tell you something, man to man. If you don't watch out, you'll grow up to be the black sheep of this entire family.

LAMBERT: You think so, Eddie?

EDDIE: I know so, pal.

LAMBERT: Yes, well, I'm going to hold onto this drawing, Eddie. So you better be nice to me tonight. And nice to me at school, too. I want to go with the gang more. When you all go to New Skateland or Crystal Beach, I want you to ask me along. And I want you to invite me for dinner so I can talk to your dad about Yale. Otherwise I'll show this around. And I don't mean just at school, either. I'll make copies of it down at the blueprint place. And I'll mail one to your parents. And another to Peggy Nussbaumer. And I'll even mail one to your grandmother.

EDDIE: That would kill her, you prick! She's got a bad heart.

LAMBERT: Then change your attitude, Eddie!

EDDIE: You know what you're doing, Lambert. You're doing blackmail! Men have died for doing that. And women, too.

END OF SCENE

Leading Ladies
Ken Ludwig

Comic

Leo and Jack, thirties to forties

Leo and Jack are two touring actors looking for their next gig. Here, they find something with potential, though they would have to become con-men to "get the job."

(The lights come up inside an empty train car, as Jack and Leo enter carrying their suitcases.)

LEO: Morons! They were complete and utter morons!

JACK: Leo —

LEO: What ever happened to respect?! Hmm? And-and-and courtesy?! I mean, didn't they even look at our flyers?! I put them in the lobby. With our best reviews! "Mesmerizing."

JACK: The Mecklenberg Ledger.

LEO: "Fascinating."

JACK: The Beaver Falls Dispatch.

LEO: *(Glares at Jack.)* "A powerhouse night of theatre." The New York Times.

JACK: You made that one up.

LEO: Yes, I know, but it was on the flyer!

JACK: Leo, do you really want to do Shakespeare all your life?

LEO: Yes! I spent three years at the Royal Academy of Dramatic Art.

JACK: You told me you went there to meet women.

LEO: I did, then I got interested. God, just look at us! It's been ten years and we're still at the bottom. Rock bottom! I can feel my arse scraping on the little stones . . .

JACK: Do you know what I want? I mean really want? *(He's deadly serious now.)* Neighbors. A house. People who care if I open the front door in the morning.

LEO: Well. . . of course . . . But Jack we can still make it! As actors! All we need is a break! *(Suddenly galvanized, turning on a dime.)* And we're in luck. Finally! This morning I read in Variety that MGM is doing a movie version of Julius Caesar. In Los Angeles. they have James Mason as Brutus, John Gielgud as Cassius, and they're looking for more Shakespearean actors. This is made for us. I mean, how many Shakespearean actors do they have in America? Six? Now, how much do we have in the kitty? For the flight — as of right now?

JACK: Leo, we can't afford it.

LEO: Don't be negative! Just tell me. How much have we saved?

JACK: You don't want to know.

LEO: A thousand? Eight hundred. Six. Five? How much?!

JACK: Nothing.

LEO: No really.

JACK: We don't have a dime.

LEO: *(In shock.)* But — but — what about last night? Our show for the moose people?

JACK: They wouldn't pay us.

LEO: What?!

JACK: I went right up to the Great Yak. He said six of his members resigned at the buffet. One more soliloquy, he would have lost the herd.

LEO: Those . . . cheaters! Those-those-those crooks.

JACK: Maybe we should do a whole play next time, like we used to.

LEO: Oh, oh, oh that's a great idea! Except we have no actors, it's just the two of us! We have seven costumes! From different plays! In a pinch we could put on "One Gentleman of Verona!" "The Taming of the Merry Wife of Windsor!"

JACK: All right, all right . . .

LEO: "Much Ado About Hamlet!"

JACK: All right!

LEO: I just . . . I . . . I mean it's . . . it's just . . .

(He's in despair. Real despair. Jack feels awful for him.)

JACK: Would you like some breakfast? Maybe they have a café car.

LEO: *(Bitterly.)* We can't afford it. Remember?

JACK: I lied. I have a dollar left. It's on me.

(Jack exits. Leo is alone and despondent. After a moment, he notices a local newspaper on the train seat across the aisle. The York Dispatch. He picks it up and glances at the front page. Then something catches his eye

and he reads more carefully. The more he reads, the more absorbed he becomes. The story continues on the inside, and when he opens the paper, we see the headline on the front page: "Oh Max, Oh Steve!" Jack re-enters.)

JACK: I can't believe it! They want a dollar-fifty for two eggs!

LEO: Jack, take a look at this.

JACK: It's highway robbery!

LEO: It's important. Look. "Oh Max, Oh Steve." "Dying Woman Seeks Loved Ones. Large Fortune At Stake." Listen! "Millionairess Florence Snider of York, Pennsylvania, is reported to be searching desperately for her sister's children, Max and Steve, to whom she intends to leave the bulk of her fortune."

JACK: I think I have some extra change some place . . .

LEO: "Miss Snider last saw Max and Steve when, as children, they sailed for England with their mother. She corresponded for a time, but then lost all contact —"

JACK: Would you get to the point, I'm hungry!

LEO: The boys went to England. They left as children. Listen: "Repeated telegrams and advertisements in America and England have failed to get a response." She can't find them! And apart from a niece named . . . Meg who lives with her in York, she wants to leave them her money.

JACK: So what?

LEO: So what?! Jack, what are we? You and I. Are we Polish?

JACK: No.

LEO: Hungarian?

JACK: No.

LEO: Lituanian?

JACK: No.

LEO: We're English! We have English accents! And look at us! We could be brothers. We even look alike. *(He holds Jack around the shoulders and they look at the audience. They look nothing at all alike, of course.)* You could be Steve and I could be Max.

JACK: Us? Her nephews?

LEO: Bingo.

JACK: But we're not her nephews. It's a lie.

LEO: Not necessarily. Do you know all your relations?

JACK: Oh, stop it. I can't pretend to be somebody else. Besides which, it's illegal. They could put us in jail!

LEO: Jack, Florence Snider has tried for months to reach her nephews and she can't find them. So we wouldn't be hurting anybody. Do you think that I would hurt anybody?

JACK: What about the niece? Meg.

LEO: The hell with her. She'll get plenty. Look, it says the estate is estimated at three million dollars. So instead of three million, she gets one million. And you get a million and I get a million.

JACK: A million dollars?

LEO: *(Emotionally.)* We could start over. Try again . . . from the beginning . . . become something . . .

JACK: Leo . . .

LEO: Jack, please.

JACK: But she could have seen pictures of her nephews! In the past couple of months!

LEO: I've thought of that, so we don't show up until she kicks the bucket.

JACK: Dead?

LEO: No, Jack, a little wooden bucket that she kicks on its side . . . Yes of course dead! We wait nearby and keep our ears to the ground. The minute she goes, we send a telegram.

JACK: It won't work.

LEO: Yes it will.

JACK: No it won't! We don't know anything about Max and Steve! How old they are. When they left. Their mother's name. Their father's name. We'd have to know somebody from York, Pennsylvania!

END OF SCENE

Life Science

Anna Ziegler

Seriocomic
Tom and Mike, teens

Mike has never initiated a conversation with Tom before; but he's threatened by Leah's interest in him. Leah is a girl Mike likes.

(Tom and Mike after practice.)

MIKE: And how unfair was it to make us run an extra mile? That's not, like nothing.

TOM: I know.

MIKE: I think Leitner's getting testy in his old age.

TOM: Totally.

MIKE: You know, I heard that Kyle's the assistant coach this year because he didn't get into college anywhere last year. He applied to like fifteen schools and nothing. Nothing.

TOM: That's awful. He must have felt —

MIKE: Scary. I know. My parents'll kill me if I don't get in anywhere. Where are you applying?

TOM: Oh. Lots of places.

MIKE: Uh-huh?

TOM: Yeah.

MIKE: Like?

TOM: Oh, like, places in the northeast mostly.

MIKE: Brandeis? You applying there?

TOM: Um, no. Not there.

MIKE: It's my first choice.

TOM: Cool.

MIKE: You're applying to like, Yale, aren't you.

TOM: Um, Mike?

MIKE: Yeah?

TOM: I was just wondering . . . like, why you're talking to me.

MIKE: Oh.

TOM: I mean.

MIKE: No. I understand. You just seem like a cool guy.

TOM: Okay.

MIKE: Are you applying to Yale?

TOM: I guess so. I mean, I may as well try.

MIKE: Well you've got a lot going for you. Asian and Jewish. You should be all set.

TOM: What does that mean?

MIKE: No, I mean. You'll get in. Everyone knows how smart you are. That's why they cheat off you . . . Dana cheats off you in math.

TOM: I don't know —

MIKE: No, she does. She sits next to you. Haven't you noticed?

TOM: I don't know. I just do my thing.

MIKE: So you're with Leah, right?

TOM: No.

MIKE: Oh.

TOM: Why?

MIKE: That's what I heard.

TOM: From who?

MIKE: From Leah.

TOM: Oh.

MIKE: Did you like, hook up?

TOM: Um, Mike —

MIKE: Sorry. I'll lay off . . . You hear about Dana's plan? She's crazy.

TOM: Yeah, I heard.

MIKE: I wondered — does it offend you?

TOM: What?

MIKE: Taking it so lightly. You know. Thinking she can change the world. Thinking certain boundaries don't apply to her.

TOM: I really don't know. I'm just . . .

MIKE: Doing your thing.

TOM: Right.

MIKE: Did anyone tell you you can be tough to talk to?

TOM: Look.

MIKE: What?

TOM: I'm shy.

MIKE: I know.

TOM: It takes me some time.

MIKE: Okay.

(Tom exits.)

END OF SCENE

Over the Tavern

Tom Dudzick

Comic
Eddie and Rudy, kids

Eddie and Rudy are brothers in a Catholic family. Here, Eddie is quizzing Rudy on his catechism.

EDDIE: *(Finds something.)* Okay, here it is. "What are the three conditions that must be present in order for a sin to be considered mortal?"

RUDY: Oh, I hate this question!

EDDIE: "First, the action must be seriously wrong or considered seriously wrong. Second, the sinner must give sufficient reflection to the serious wrong. Third, the sinner must have full consent of the will."

RUDY: They really know how to take the fun out of sinning.

EDDIE: *(Slams book to the floor.)* Why can't they say it in English?

RUDY: Careful! *(Runs for book.)*

EDDIE: How am I supposed to know if it was seriously wrong? They think everything is serious.

RUDY: Well, if you're so worried, go to confession.

EDDIE: I'm not telling this to a priest! *(Thinks hard.)* Except if I die with a mortal sin on my soul I go to Hell. But if it was only venial, I just go to Purgatory. *(Grabs book from Rudy:)* Is there fire in Purgatory? *(Quickly finds something:)* Okay, there's fire. But it's not as hot as Hell.

RUDY: Where does it say?

EDDIE: There's pictures. The flames are smaller.

RUDY: *(Looks:)* That's a drawing.

EDDIE: Whattaya think, they take cameras to Hell?

RUDY: Well anyway, maybe there is no Hell.

EDDIE: *(Stunned, he runs and shuts the door.)* Are you completely nuts?! Saying something like that out loud?!

RUDY: It was just an idea.

EDDIE: Public school kids have those ideas. That's why they're there. 'Cause they're gonna wind up in Hell anyway!

RUDY: Aw, man! I'm gonna start my own religion. No uniforms, no catechism and no rules — except you *have* to eat spaghetti on Friday. Pazinski-ism!

EDDIE: *(Awed:)* Man, Satan's having your room painted right now!

RUDY: What was your impure thought about?

EDDIE: None of your bees wax!

RUDY: Just give me the subject matter.

EDDIE: Well . . . I guess that'd be alright. Okay, Vinny Carducci said —

RUDY: Who's Vinny Carducci?

EDDIE: Who cares? He's new, I haven't met him yet. So, Vinny Carducci told Iggy Sabadasz that there's this girl around here who leaves her shade up at night and gets *bare* in front of her window! *("Bare" is sotto voice.)*

RUDY: Who! Who is it?

EDDIE: That's the thing, Carducci won't tell.

RUDY: Did you see her?

EDDIE: No, stupid, I'm telling you, I only had the impure thought! Now shut up, will ya? This is Hell we're talking about! I gotta think! *(Racks his brain:)* . . . Seriously wrong . . . Full consent of the will.

RUDY: Wait, that's it!

EDDIE: What?

RUDY: You didn't have full consent of the will! Vinny's description of the girl in the window was so good that you became, like . . . possessed by Satan!

EDDIE: Yeah! Yeah! Beautiful!

RUDY: *(Laughs:)* I can't believe they let you into high school with that brain!

EDDIE: *(Calmly:)* Y'know, you're right. I need to study more. *(Starts to rip page from book:)* Like this page right here . . .

RUDY: Hey, cut it out! I'll get killed for that!

EDDIE: Get away!

RUDY: I gotta take that to school, stop it!

EDDIE: Beat it!

RUDY: Stop it, will ya?

(Eddie folds the page and pockets it; he tosses the book aside. Rudy picks up book and examines the damage, holding back tears.)

RUDY: Why'd you do that?

EDDIE: I felt like it.

RUDY: I was helping you.

EDDIE: So?

RUDY: You always do that. You pretend to be friends with me, then do something rotten.

EDDIE: So?

RUDY: I hate you!

EDDIE: Ooh, wow.

RUDY: *(Beats his pillow with his fist:)* I hate you, I hate you, I hate you, I hate you!

EDDIE: I'll live.

RUDY: Alright, then, here goes. I didn't want to tell you this, but you made me. *Daddy traded your good comic books to Green Teeth Malicki!*

EDDIE: Yeah, right.

RUDY: He did!

EDDIE: Nobody's that stupid. Nice try, though.

END OF SCENE

They're Just Like Us
Boo Killebrew

Dramatic
Gene and Frank, twenties

Gene and Frank are constantly trying to come up with new ways to get attention.

GENE: Hey.
FRANK: Hey.
GENE: You going somewhere?
FRANK: No. You?
GENE: No.
FRANK: You've been around a lot more lately.
GENE: Yeah.
FRANK: It was really great to see you at the Outer Space Birthday Party.
GENE: Yeah.
FRANK: Are you finished with all of your secret stuff?
GENE: Oh, all that stuff I was doing?
FRANK: Yeah.
GENE: Yeah, that's done.
FRANK: What was it?
GENE: I really don't want to get into it.
FRANK: Gene!
GENE: I'm sorry, Frank, it's a long story and it's weird and complicated.
FRANK: You said that once it was done you would tell me about it.
GENE: I know and I will one of these days. I just need some time away from it. I need some time to think about it before I really start talking about it.
FRANK: Gene.
GENE: I'm sorry, Frank. Please understand I just need some time to let it rest.
FRANK: Are you okay?

GENE: I will be. Are you okay?

FRANK: Yeah.

GENE: I mean, are you okay about the big breakup?

FRANK: Oh. You heard about that?

GENE: Yeah, it was impossible not to. I mean, I was at Marty's party when it happened.

FRANK: Yeah.

GENE: You caught him with that cross-eyed actor from "Divine Justice" in the moonwalk, right?

FRANK: Yeah, I did, Gene. I'm okay and I'm actually ready for the whole thing to be over.

GENE: I thought it was over.

FRANK: Well, Mickey and I are completely over. I'm just ready for everyone to stop talking about it.

GENE: Yeah.

FRANK: It was just such a huge drama, the whole thing. I'm done with it.

GENE: Yeah.

FRANK: I'm going to do whatever it takes so that in the future, people aren't paying so much attention to me and my relationships. It's impossible to function like that.

GENE: It's very hard.

FRANK: It's very, very hard.

GENE: Trust me, I know.

FRANK: What?

GENE: I know. *(Looks at Frank.)* Trust me.

FRANK: Okay.

GENE: Yep.

FRANK: I just couldn't take it anymore. I need to be with someone where there is no drama, no scandal. I need to be with a nice, normal someone who lives in the country and has a dog or something.

GENE: Yeah.

FRANK: I can't even watch "Divine Justice" without feeling sick to my stomach.

GENE: I'm so sorry.

FRANK: Thanks.

(Pause.)

GENE: So did you hear about Jen?

FRANK: How she was hospitalized for exhaustion?

GENE: Yeah.

FRANK: Yeah. Did you know she's in rehab now?

GENE: No way!

FRANK: Isn't that terrible?

GENE: Yeah, what for?

FRANK: Well, everyone says it's because of an eating disorder, but I think she also is probably in because of her tendency to take a little beak lunch every now and then.

GENE: Jen does coke?

FRANK: And then some.

GENE: Wow, I never knew Jen was such a —

FRANK: Rebellious soul?

GENE: Yeah.

FRANK: Yeah. I think she does all this because she's hiding some deep hurt that she has within her.

GENE: Wow, I guess there is a lot more to Jen than I thought.

FRANK: Yeah.

GENE: You talked to her?

FRANK: Yeah, she said she was okay and that she wanted everyone to stop talking about it.

GENE: I don't really think anyone is talking about it.

FRANK: Really?

GENE: Well, with your breakup and Marty's big party and Ann in Africa — I don't know, no one is really talking about Jen and her little stint at rehab.

FRANK: Well, that's good. I'll let her know, she'll be happy to hear that.

GENE: Yeah. She's doing okay now?

FRANK: I think so. Jen has tons of people that love her and will take good care of her.

GENE: Okay.

(Pause.)

FRANK: Do you know if Ann is back from Africa? I heard she might be getting back today.

GENE: I don't know.

FRANK: Yeah, no one has really said anything to me about it.

GENE: I should email her.

FRANK: I should too. Maybe she is back and she's been too busy with the baby to update her MySpace blog.

GENE: Yeah, I feel bad, spending time in impoverished African countries can really haunt a person for the rest of their life.

FRANK: What?

GENE: Impoverished African countries. Trust me, I know.

FRANK: I hear that.

FRANK: *(Looks at his watch.)* I gotta run, but I'll email Ann and I'll let you know if she's back and what the deal is with the baby.

GENE: If I get a chance, I'm gonna try to email too.

FRANK: I'll text you and let you know what I find out.

GENE: I'll do the same.

FRANK: Bye.

GENE: Bye!

END OF SCENE

Scenes for Two Women

All This Intimacy

Rajiv Joseph

Seriocomic
Jen and Franny, twenties

Ty is a guy who has gotten three women pregnant, one of whom is his actual girlfriend Jen. Here, her sister Franny is counseling her.

PICTURE OF HAPPINESS

(Franny's kitchen.)

JEN: Just give me your blessing, okay?

FRANNY: Oh. You want a *blessing*? Fuck that. I'm not blessing shit. No bless. No bless from me.

JEN: Fine, don't bless.

FRANNY: I'm not.

JEN: Don't then.

FRANNY: Fine.

JEN: Fine.

(Beat.)

FRANNY: *(Whines.)* Jen . . .

JEN: *(Mock whines.)* Franny . . .

FRANNY: I'm just saying.

Why? Why *this particular* . . .

(She gestures to Jen's womb.)

The last thing you want is Ty's kid.

His *offspring*.

JEN: It's how the cookie's crumbled.

FRANNY: Wrong! That's wrong and wrong-headed and you're doing this for the wrong reasons!

JEN: You don't know why —

FRANNY: — Defeatist. You're being defeatist.

JEN: No. I'm being optimistic. Life. Newness. Baby. Okay?

FRANNY: That's like the stupidest thing I've ever heard you say in my entire life. What about school?

JEN: What about it?

FRANNY: Jen, you're like the smartest person in the world. You have every degree known to man.

JEN: And? And what? What do I have to show for it? Why do you think I've been in school so long?

FRANNY: I don't know Jen. You love to read.

You need therapy. Not a baby.

JEN: I'm embracing life!

FRANNY: Who don't you embrace my ass!

JEN: Franny . . . I understand that you want the best for me, but what I'd really like is to go eat. I want lunch. I want phad thai.

FRANNY: You're going to be *7 months pregnant* for my wedding. *Showing!*

JEN: So? I'll make you look skinny.

FRANNY: I —

What?

JEN: What?

FRANNY: So I look *fat?*

JEN: That's not what I —

FRANNY: Oh that is low.

JEN: Fran, that's not —

FRANNY: Fine, go ahead! Get pregnant and get fat and be a fatty.

JEN: Fine! I will!

FRANNY: Fine!

(Beat.)

FRANNY: You're going to ruin my wedding pictures.

What's it going to be like? How is that going to feel to be all bloated up in front of everyone — in front of Grandma and Grandpa?

JEN: I can deal with it.

FRANNY: And what are you going to say when they ask you who the father is?

JEN: I don't know. I'll tell them it's the best man.

FRANNY: No you won't. If you think Ty is still Seth's best man, you're crazy.

JEN: Why, what happened now?

FRANNY: Ty just got uninvited to the wedding.

JEN: You can't do that. He's Seth's best friend.

FRANNY: I can do whatever I want. It's my wedding.
Ty is OUT and Paco is IN.

JEN: Paco?

FRANNY: Seth's new best man. It was my idea.

JEN: He's ten years old!

FRANNY: He's twelve. And his English is getting better.

JEN: *Paco?*

FRANNY: He'll be adorable. He's a splash of color.

JEN: You're nuts.

FRANNY: But you . . . Jen, my big sis . . . I don't want you to be pregnant in my wedding pictures. We'll have to get your dress altered and you'll be huge and everything. I just don't want to have to explain you every time I show the pictures to someone.

JEN: What is your fixation with these wedding pictures?

FRANNY: It's not a fixation. It's —

JEN: Yes it is. Every time you open your mouth, you talk about your wedding pictures. You're obsessed or something. Stupid photographs.

FRANNY: They're not stupid.
(Beat.)
Why would you say that? They're not stupid.

JEN: *Stupid.* Stupid *pictures.* No one ever looks at wedding pictures. You know why? They're stupid.

FRANNY: No! You're so negative! Anything that's important to me, you have to shit all over!

JEN: I'm looking for a little support and all you can talk about is how I'm going to look in your stupid wedding pictures.
(Beat.)

FRANNY: I have Mom and Dad's wedding pictures.

JEN: *What?*

FRANNY: Mom gave them to me.

JEN: I don't believe you. Let me see them.

FRANNY: Mom gave them to me.

JEN: Even if they *did* have pictures Mom would have burned them.

FRANNY: Well she didn't.

JEN: So let's see them.

FRANNY: Oh you want to *see* them?

JEN: Yeah.

FRANNY: Why? They're *stupid.* They're just stupid *pictures.*

JEN: There are no pictures. And Mom would never give you something like that.

(Franny goes to a drawer and pulls a large photo out.)

FRANNY: Here it is.

JEN: One? One picture.

FRANNY: Mom and Dad on their wedding day.

(Looking at it.)

So happy. So full of hope.

JEN: Let me see it.

FRANNY: No.

JEN: Franny —

FRANNY: *(Mocking.) . . . Jen . . .*

JEN: *(Losing it.) Let me see the fucking picture!*

(Franny hands Jen the picture.)

FRANNY: Here. Spaz.

(Jen looks at the picture. Long beat. She's never seen it or anything like it. She feels about 10 different emotions at once.)

JEN: *(Gasp.)*

FRANNY: I know, right?

JEN: I mean . . . This is . . .

Look at this.

(Franny and Jen look at the picture together.)

JEN: I can't believe you have this.

Look at them.

FRANNY: I know.

JEN: I mean, Look at them, Fran.

(They look at the picture for a beat.)

FRANNY: I know.

(Jen puts the picture down.)

JEN: But it's folly, you know.

FRANNY: It's what?

JEN: Folly.

FRANNY: What the fuck is folly?

JEN: It's just —

FRANNY: What is that, like garnish at Christmas?

JEN: No, that's "Holly." Folly is —

FRANNY: No, forget it! I don't want to know. With your stupid SAT words and everything.

(Mimicking Jen.)

It's *Folly.* Fuck that! Fuck Folly.

JEN: All I'm saying is it's not real! It's just an image!

FRANNY: Oh, is that all?

JEN: Yes.

FRANNY: That's all you're saying?

JEN: Jesus, Fran, yes.

FRANNY: Well, all *I'm* saying is you're going to be fat and bloated and ugly at my wedding and if I want to airbrush your fat stomach out of my wedding pictures I will!

END OF SCENE

BFF
Kathryn Walat

Dramatic
Lauren and Elizabeth, both twelve, played by actresses in their twenties

Lauren and Eliza are "best friends forever," here wondering what it will be like to be adults.

(Lauren, twelve, is swimming in a pool. She gets out and dries herself off. Eliza, twelve, is lying on a towel, reading a magazine. It's summer; the sun is bright. Lauren is in a bikini. Eliza wears a t-shirt and eats, intermittently, from a box of cereal. Lauren lies down, her head on Eliza's stomach. They lie in this position for a little while before speaking.)

LAUREN: Liza, what do you think it'll be like to be grown up?

ELIZA: I don't know.

LAUREN: I mean, do you think it feels different than this?

(Eliza thinks about it.)

ELIZA: No. Probably not.

LAUREN: Right. Probably not.

ELIZA: Why do you ask?

LAUREN: I don't know.

ELIZA: Okay.

LAUREN: No, I mean, I just got this feeling, while I was swimming, that the years are gonna pass so quickly.

ELIZA: Oh . . . I don't want them to.

LAUREN: This feeling that everything happens at once, you know? That we're already grown up and walking around somewhere and doing some job and we just don't know it.

ELIZA: You're not making sense, Lauren.

LAUREN: I am.

ELIZA: Okay.

LAUREN: Let's make something up.

ELIZA: Okay.

LAUREN: Let's tell the future.
ELIZA: I don't want to think about the future.
LAUREN: Like, where are we gonna live?
ELIZA: I don't know —
LAUREN: New York City?
ELIZA: Yeah, I guess.
LAUREN: We could have, like, apartments next to each other.
ELIZA: *(Finally getting into it a little.)* We could live in the same apartment.
LAUREN: Absolutely.

(Beat.)

Will we get married?

ELIZA: To each other?
LAUREN: No! I meant, in general.
ELIZA: I think we will. When we want to.
LAUREN: How will we know when we want to?
ELIZA: I don't know. I guess when the right person comes along.
LAUREN: But who will the right person be?
ELIZA: Really nice.
LAUREN: Eliza.
ELIZA: What?
LAUREN: He's gotta be hot.
ELIZA: Of course hot. I meant hot too. Nice and hot.
LAUREN: And funny.
ELIZA: It would be great if he were funny. *(Beat.)* And he should have a secret.
LAUREN: What do you mean?
ELIZA: Something he only tells you.
LAUREN: I guess. Yeah.
ELIZA: He'll be shy but also open. A little awkward but in a sweet way.

(Long beat.)

ELIZA: But do you ever get the feeling of missing someone even when you're sitting right next to them?
LAUREN: Liza —
ELIZA: I miss you.

(Beat.)

LAUREN: I'm sorry.
ELIZA: About what?
LAUREN: I don't know.

END OF SCENE

BFF
Kathryn Walat

Dramatic
Lauren, twenties
Megan, twenties

(Lauren is all alone in the large empty yoga room. She is sitting in the middle of the floor, not moving. After a long while, a woman, played by the same actress as Eliza, enters.)

MEGAN: Oh! I'm sorry. I'm interrupting —

(Beat.)

Are you okay?

(Beat. Lauren doesn't even look up.)

If you want, I can leave. There might be another open room. If you want privacy.

LAUREN: *(Quietly, meaning "please leave.")* It's fine.

MEGAN: *(Not getting it at all.)* Okay!

(Megan spreads out her mat.)

I guess you're having a rough day too. I know I shouldn't say it; we've barely just met, but you'd think by my age, I'd have found a way to get over PMS, huh?? But no. I'm as pissed off as ever. *(Beat.)* Now you definitely want me to leave, right? What an introduction. Megan.

LAUREN: What?

MEGAN: My name. Megan. And you? Do you have one?

LAUREN: Eliza.

MEGAN: No, you don't look like an Eliza. It's funny. I guess I knew one once.

LAUREN: *(More to herself.)* I did too.

MEGAN: I just started yoga. I find it incredibly calming. My therapist says I talk so much that I need to find something I can do in silence. So what do I do? I find you! There were other empty rooms. Don't tell.

LAUREN: Okay.

MEGAN: It just seemed so much nicer than going to the gym. I hate those machines, the way you strap in and stay there for forty-five minutes. It's like your brain's on hold while your body sweats. It's unnatural.

LAUREN: *(After a breath.)* I can't stand gyms.

MEGAN: This is the closest I could come. I like to take walks, really. But my doctor doesn't think it's cardiovascular enough. *(Beat.)* Let me know if you want me to be quiet. I can do that. I am capable.

(Long beat.)

I mean, it's been such a day already. What a breath of fresh air, huh? Just chatting. I swear, if I have to look another woman in the eye and ask her whether she's menstruating. God help me.

(Beat. Lauren stares at her.)

No — I'm a nurse. A nurse. *(Beat.)* What a world, eh?

LAUREN: Yeah.

MEGAN: How about you? What do you do?

LAUREN: I work with aquatic animals.

MEGAN: You're a marine biologist?

LAUREN: That's right.

MEGAN: You like the water?

LAUREN: Yes, I guess so.

MEGAN: I hate it. Refused to learn to swim when I was a girl. All I would do was stand on the first step of the pool or in the shallowest part of the ocean and stare out at the deep. It seemed so daunting. And to this day, I won't put my whole head in. I like being able to breathe. Without breath, how do you feel alive, right?

LAUREN: In school, senior year of high school, I won the contest for staying longest underwater.

MEGAN: How long?

LAUREN: Oh, I think I nearly died. However long is almost too long.

MEGAN: Good lord. You and I are not the same.

LAUREN: You know, a man proposed to me the other day. *(Beat.)* I don't know why I'm telling you, but —

MEGAN: No, I love this stuff. Eat it up. What'd you say?

LAUREN: Well, I took off.

MEGAN: Oh honey. You don't love him?

LAUREN: I don't know.

MEGAN: I was once in a relationship with a man, let's call him Gus. He used to take me places, to parks, to sit in empty pews of churches at midnight, to late night movies, to small towns upstate. He was so good to me. Romantic, you know, and like I said I'm not very . . . romantic, just a late-bloomer I guess, and after awhile I got wary of all the nice things he did. They started seeming more . . . I don't know, manipulative than they really were. I stopped sleeping with him. Soon, we didn't even kiss. He moved to Vermont, I think, or maybe Maine? And I heard recently that he got married. You know how it goes.

LAUREN: Were you sad?

MEGAN: Yes.

(Beat.)

But did I have a right to be? There I'm not so sure.

LAUREN: I think you had a right to be.

MEGAN: Yeah? Well . . . Life's so hard. One can't always blame oneself. We make so many decisions, some are bound to be wrong.

LAUREN: You know . . . you remind me of someone. It's incredible, really.

MEGAN: Is that right?

LAUREN: Like a friend I once had —

MEGAN: All my life people have told me that. That I seem like someone else.

LAUREN: I miss her.

MEGAN: Who?

LAUREN: Eliza.

MEGAN: You have the same name? Cute.

LAUREN: No — I mean, yes. The same name. Had.

MEGAN: Was she nice?

LAUREN: Of course. I mean, she was very nice.

MEGAN: No one's very nice. Some people pass themselves off as nice tolerably well but we're animals, all of us.

LAUREN: No, she was . . . she didn't have a cruel bone in her body.

MEGAN: She did. She hated people. She probably hated you for a while.

LAUREN: But I deserved it.

MEGAN: She thought you were mean.

LAUREN: And I am.

MEGAN: You were in school. You were a child . . .You know, I went into a lot of people's private yoga rooms and no one else said a word to me.

LAUREN: What are you talking about? What do you mean I was a child —

MEGAN: I sensed, even then, that . . .

LAUREN: That what?

MEGAN: You were a good person. I deal with so many people in the course of a day — people in less pain than you and they're unashamed about being malicious.

LAUREN: No. I promise you. I guarantee you. I'm not at all good —

MEGAN: You've been through the mill.

LAUREN: Who are you?

MEGAN: Who are you?

LAUREN: I'm . . .

MEGAN: You're wonderful.

LAUREN: That's what Seth says. I don't know what he sees in me.

MEGAN: He's lonely. He's reached the end of being alone. And he has nice hair — the way it sticks up a little, like an alien.

LAUREN: Eliza?

MEGAN: *(Standing to leave.)* Megan. I'm sorry — maybe I should go.

LAUREN: No!

MEGAN: You know, in my experience, life is what you make of it. If you decide you like gray days, then you like gray days. They're transformed.

LAUREN: But —

MEGAN: Right after my father died, when I was eleven, I told my mother that I wished she were dead too. We had a fight about R-rated movies; she didn't want me to go to a party where they would be watching *Pretty Woman* even though it was my best friend's party, and I said that awful thing and then she cried in a way she'd never cried before, not even after my father died.

LAUREN: You were upset.

MEGAN: But I said it. And at the time, I meant it.

LAUREN: Did you apologize?

MEGAN: Never. But my mother knew it wasn't how I really felt. She forgave me.

LAUREN: Oh God. Eliza?
MEGAN: No, there is no God.
LAUREN: This is a dream.
MEGAN: Then wake up.
LAUREN: I can't.
MEGAN: You can.

END OF SCENE

Bhutan
Daisy Foote

Dramatic
Mary and Sara, late thirties

Mary and Sara are sisters. Mary is a widow. Sara is a heavy drinker. Neither has a man in her life.

(Saturday night, the evening of Warren's eighteenth birthday. Mary and Sara, quite drunk, stumble into the kitchen. They are giggling and carry Mrs. Letemkin's lawn signs.)

MARY: What the hell are we going to do with these?
SARA: Burn them.
MARY: NOW?!
(Sara grabs the signs from Mary.)
SARA: No. Tomorrow. Over to my house. Let's hide them for now.
(Sara hides them behind the refrigerator.)
(Mary plops into a chair.)
MARY: Shit . . . I'm wasted.
(Sara lights a joint, they pass it back and forth.)
MARY: *(Continued.)* So what did you say to Carl?
SARA: How's work? Your truck holding up okay? How about them Red Sox?
(Mary and Sara collapse into giggles.)
MARY: He couldn't take his eyes off you.
SARA: Shut up.
MARY: He was staring at your boobs.
(This gets them laughing again.)
SARA: He said he missed me.
(Mary laughs.)
SARA: *(Continued.)* And I said . . . "Too fucking bad. Tell it to your wife."
(More laughter.)
SARA: *(Continued.)* I never thought he'd do it . . . marry someone else. I thought maybe he'd date her for awhile, wave her around in front

of our friends, try and make me jealous. But marry her . . . some woman he barely knew two weeks . . . when we'd been together for fifteen years? Why'd he do that?

MARY: You said no.

(They drink their beers and then a loud banging starts.)

SARA: What the hell is that?

MARY: The furnace.

SARA: Jesus . . .

MARY: I told you.

(The banging stops.)

SARA: I thought the whole house was going to blow.

(Silence. They drink and pass the joint.)

MARY: I wonder what Warren is doing right now?

SARA: Probably having sex with Anna . . . happy birthday.

MARY: If Charlie were here it wouldn't be like this. Charlie would talk to Warren. He would have told him, stay away from her. You'll never be happy with a girl like that.

SARA: What kind of girl would he be happy with?

MARY: I don't know. But Charlie would have known. A boy is lost without his father.

SARA: Warren doesn't seem lost to me.

MARY: What the hell do you know about it? You're not his mother? I'm his mother and believe me, he's lost.

(Mary gets another beer.)

SARA: Don't I get one of those?

MARY: Get one yourself.

(Sara goes to the refrigerator for a beer.)

MARY: *(Continued.)* I was a terrible wife.

SARA: You were not.

MARY: I was yelling at Charlie, telling him he needed to do more, telling him I wasn't happy.

SARA: Sometimes you weren't happy.

MARY: What the hell does that mean?

SARA: I mean the guy wasn't perfect.

MARY: He was good in the sack.

SARA: Oh Jesus . . .

MARY: You tell me I should go out and have sex with other guys . . .

SARA: Well you should. You're thirty-eight years old, you could have another kid if you wanted to.

MARY: Joe White.

SARA: What?

MARY: A few days after Charlie died, I never told you. Joe White came up to the house. You'd taken the kids to McDonalds. And Joe . . . Joe came over. He was shit faced. Crying and crying about Charlie. His best friend. His partner. His brother. "What are we going to do without Charlie, Mary?" Over and over he kept asking me. And the next thing I know, he's kissing me.

SARA: Joe White?

MARY: He had his hands all over me. And his tongue in my mouth. And for a minute, you know, for a minute I was letting him do it. But then he lets out this burp. I guess it was all the beer he'd been drinking. And when he did that, I could taste all the onions he'd been eating earlier. Then I just wanted him off of me. I wanted him out of the house and the kids home and sleeping in their beds. So I kicked him, I kicked him in the balls.

SARA: What the hell did he do?

MARY: He threw up. And he ran out of the house. Never mentioned it again. I never mentioned it again. Two months later he was married to Doreen.

SARA: It wouldn't be like that with another guy?

MARY: How do you know that?

SARA: There are no guarantees. But it could be really great. You could have great sex.

MARY: No . . . no one could be better than Charlie.

SARA: What if they were better?

(Mary is suddenly screaming at her.)

MARY: He was my husband, you don't talk like that about him in this house . . . his house.

. . .

SARA: This isn't Charlie's house. It was Dad's house . . . and his father's house and his father's father's house. And the only reason you got it was because you were older and had kids.

(Mary starts to yell again.)

MARY: A lightning bolt. A goddamn lightning bolt shoots out of the sky and kills my husband. All because some flatlander can't live without his Jacuzzi and view of the mountains.

SARA: Shower . . . it was a shower. One of those triple headed deals.

MARY: Don't tell me what my husband was or wasn't installing when he was struck down by lightning . .

SARA: Big enough for three people, he was sitting on the bench, fiddling with the pipe, when the lightning traveled . . .

MARY: It was a Jacuzzi and he was underneath the deck. I was so mad at him.

END OF SCENE

Dog Sees God: Confessions of a Teenaged Blockhead

Bert V. Royal

Comic
Tricia and Marcy, teens

This play imagines what the characters from "Peanuts" might be like as teenagers. Here, Tricia and Marcy are having lunch in the school cafeteria.

SPORK

(Cafeteria. Lunchtime. Two girls, Tricia and Marcy, enter with their lunch trays and take a seat at an empty table.)

TRICIA: So, he was all like, "Woh woh woh. Woh woh. Woh woh woh wowoh woh." He is such a dick! So, I'm like: "Excuse me, Mr. Von Pffefferkorn, but just because I can't define metaphor doesn't mean I don't know what one is, you stupid buttwad!"

MARCY: You called Mr. Von Pffefferkorn a buttwad?!

TRICIA: No, of course not. I added that to the story for dramatic effect.

MARCY: Oh.

TRICIA: I begged and pleaded to God not to put me in his class. I wanted to be in Mr. Griffin's lit class. He gives A's to anyone with tits. But, no, I get the fag.

MARCY: Do you really think Mr. Von Pfefferkorn is a fag?

TRICIA: Well, if he were straight, then obviously I wouldn't be failing his class.

MARCY: Totally!

TRICIA: The thing is: I really think that God is punishing me for sleeping with Fatty-fat Frieda's boyfriend.

MARCY: You slept with Craig Kovelsky?!

TRICIA: I blew him. You knew that! I totally told you right after it happened!

MARCY: You did not!!

TRICIA: I so did!

MARCY: Ewwwww!

TRICIA: I was drunk, okay? Speaking of, is anybody looking??

MARCY: No, sir.

TRICIA: *(Condescendingly.)* Sweetie, you're gotta stop calling me that. *(Over the following dialogue, Tricia reaches into her backpack and produces a large bottle of vodka. She pours a large amount into her milk carton, she passes it to Marcy, who does the same. Tricia quickly puts the bottle back into her backpack. Marcy produces a bottle of Kahlua from her backpack, and they repeat this action. They take their cartons, close them and shake vigorously, in unison. Switching gears:)* I think I did it, subconsciously, just because I fucking hate Frieda Fatass.

MARCY: Oh my God! I know, right?!

TRICIA: Totally right! I mean, seriously, whenever one of us is upset over a real problem, she has to butt her fat ass in and start crying about how she can't stop puking up her food.

MARCY: It's soooo pathetic!

TRICIA: I swear to God, if I have to hear her bitch one more time about how Craig won't sleep with her until she loses weight, I'm going to stick my foot up her ass. That is, if I can find the entrance. If she's bulimic, will someone please tell me why she's such a heifer? I mean, come on, Frieda.

MARCY: She told me the other day she was on a diet and I was thinking, like: What? You can't eat anything larger than your head? Survey says —

MARCY AND TRICIA: YOU'RE FAT!

MARCY: Take your finger out of your throat and drag your ass to Lane Bryant.

TRICIA: And speaking of her fashion sense, why is she always wearing that shirt that says WWJD? What the hell is that supposed to mean? Who wants jelly doughnuts? *(Marcy spits her drink all over the place.)*

MARCY: *(Laughing.)* I think it's: What would Jesus do.

TRICIA: Well, He wouldn't wear that ugly-ass shirt with those nasty-ass spandex shorts. SPANDEX! Who wears Spandex?!

MARCY: Somebody needs to explain "camel toe" to her.

TRICIA: Her body is so gross! *(Imitating Frieda.)* "I'm not just the president of the Itty Bitty Titty Committee; I'm also a client!" Blecch! "What would Jesus do?"

MARCY: He wouldn't let Darryl Farmer finger Him under the bleachers during a pep rally, that's for damn sure!

TRICIA: Totally! Now, what should we drink to?

MARCY: How about "life, liberty and the pursuit of happiness"?

TRICIA: Marcy, I hate to tell you this. But sometimes you are really bland.

MARCY: Screw you! I am not.

TRICIA: Well, hello!!! There's a thousand things in this world to toast to and you pick the lamest one ever!

MARCY: Okay. Here's to . . . *(Looking down at her tray.)* Tater tots.

TRICIA: Well, that's slightly more interesting. *(They "clink" cartons and down their drinks.)*

MARCY: I'm buzzed.

TRICIA: Me too. *(They stare at their plates. Tricia picks up her spork and studies it.)* The spork is a great invention. Simple, but effective. It's like, who came up with it? *(Tricia makes them another round.)*

MARCY: The spork was invented in the 1940s. After the war, when the U.S. Army occupied Japan, General MacArthur decreed that the use of chopsticks was uncivilized, and the conquered should use forks and spoons like — quote — the civilized world. But fearing that the Japanese might rise up, revolt and retake their country with their forks, he and the U.S. Army invented the much less dangerous spork, which was then introduced into the public schools. But really all a spork is, is a plastic descendant of the runcible spoon. *(Tricia is shocked.)*

TRICIA: Okay. Umm. How did you know that?

MARCY: Can you keep a secret?

TRICIA: Can Frieda eat a moon pie in only two bites?

MARCY: No. Seriously. I'm the smartest person in the world.

TRICIA: Yeah. And she's the skinniest.

MARCY: No, it's true. I was part of this government experiment in elementary school. It was a drug that made kids, like, super geniuses. Able to retain everything they learned. But the drug had a side effect . . .

TRICIA: *(Without missing a beat.)* Backne?

MARCY: Shut up, bitch! You know I'm sensitive about that!

TRICIA: I am not sorry, girlfriend. Why don't you just go to the damn dermatologist?

MARCY: *(Annoyed.)* Can I please finish my story? So this miracle super genius drug fucks with all the kids' hormones and turns everybody into, like, horny children. Like, all these third graders are running around humping, like, everything. *(Tricia is dumbfounded by this information.)*

TRICIA: That is so weird! You WERE really smart when we were kids! And really horny . . . *(Marcy bursts out laughing.)*

MARCY: Got you! Ha ha! You're so fucking gullible!

TRICIA: You're a snatch!

MARCY: You'll believe anything.

TRICIA: How did you know all that stuff about the spork?

MARCY: Duh! I looked it up on the Internet. Every time we do get drunk at school, you pick up a spork and say, "The spork is such a great invention. I wonder where it came from." So, I decided that I was going to be ready one day with the answer.

TRICIA: *(Sarcastically.)* How brilliant of you. *(There is a moment of silence. They both finish off their drinks. Tricia turns hers over and nothing comes out. She pulls the bottle of vodka out of her bag and pours a shitload of it into the empty milk carton. Marcy slides her carton over and Tricia refills hers, as well. They both begin to down the vodka.)* I'm depressed. *(They look at each other and break out into inebriated laughter.)*

END OF SCENE

Life Science

Anna Ziegler

Dramatic
Dana and Leah, teens

Dana says she plans to adopt a Lebanese boy, but Leah thinks these plans have more to do with being rejected by Mike, her ex-boyfriend, than with a genuine desire to care for a child. She doesn't say so, though; not yet.

(Dana and Leah. After school, at Dana's house.)

DANA: So I heard back from the TV producer guy. He like wants to talk to me, to set up a meeting.
LEAH: Does he know how old you are?
DANA: I don't think that's important.
LEAH: Dana.
DANA: He emailed me more photos of Abdul. Leah, he's so beautiful, and so sad.
LEAH: Why don't you talk to your parents?
DANA: Oh, I did. I did.
LEAH: What did they say?
DANA: They said sure.
LEAH: So they'll adopt him?
DANA: Well, officially, but I'll take care of him.
LEAH: Does he even speak English?
DANA: Oh. I don't know. But I could teach him. I'll teach him English!
LEAH: So things with Tom are progressing.
DANA: Now he's your boyfriend?
LEAH: Oh, um, no. Not technically.
DANA: I think Abdul will like the upstairs room overlooking the pool. What do you think?

LEAH: I don't know what Abdul will like.

DANA: Well, he's been used to like, what, desert? It must be very dry in Lebanon —

LEAH: Beirut's a city, Dana. There's probably Starbucks there.

DANA: I want to give him a sense of space.

LEAH: Maryland doesn't have any space, Dana. It's like, crowded.

DANA: I guess.

LEAH: So Tom said that Mike was talking about you.

DANA: Oh yeah?

LEAH: He thinks this adoption thing is crazy. He thinks you're off your rocker.

DANA: Well I'm not.

LEAH: And Dana . . . I think so too. And so does Tom.

DANA: Why does what Tom thinks matter? Everyone knows you really like Mike but because he went out with me for so long you can't go for him now because he's my leftovers.

LEAH: I don't like Mike.

DANA: Since when?

LEAH: What are you, Himmler?

DANA: What are you talking about?

LEAH: You're like, questioning me, aggressively.

DANA: You're weird.

LEAH: When I got back from Poland, I just didn't like him anymore, okay? I don't know why.

DANA: I know why.

LEAH: You do?

DANA: Either you realize now, after what he did to me, that he's an asshole, or . . .

LEAH: What?

DANA: You're shunning the Jews.

LEAH: I am?

DANA: You're afraid of us.

LEAH: That's ridiculous.

DANA: Is it?

LEAH: Yes.

DANA: You don't want to be Jewish anymore. You've said as much.

LEAH: Being scared of something doesn't mean you're going to shun it.

DANA: So you're afraid of who you are?

LEAH: I guess so.

DANA: That's okay. So am I.

END OF SCENE

Poof
Lynn Nottage

Comic
Loureen and Florence, thirties

Loureen's husband Samuel has just gone up in smoke in the kitchen, as she explains to her friend Florence.

LOUREEN: *(In the darkness:)* DAMN YOU TO HELL, SAMUEL!
(A bright flash. Lights rise. A huge pile of smoking ashes rests in the middle of the kitchen. Loureen, a demure housewife in her early thirties, stares down at the ashes incredulously. She bends and lifts a pair of spectacles from the remains. She ever so slowly back away.)

LOUREEN: Samuel? Uh! *(Places the spectacles on the kitchen table.)* Uh! . . . Samuel? *(Looks around.)* Don't fool with me now. I'm not in the mood. *(Whispers:)* Samuel? I didn't mean it really. I'll be good if you come back . . . Come on now, dinner's waiting. *(Chuckles, then stops abruptly.)* Now stop your foolishness . . . And let's sit down. *(Examines the spectacles.)* Uh! *(Softly:)* Don't be cross with me. Sure I forgot to pick up your shirt for tomorrow. I can wash another, I'll do it right now. Right now! Sam? . . . *(Cautiously:)* You hear me! *(Awaits a response.)* Maybe I didn't ever intend to wash your shirt. *(Pulls back as though about to receive a blow; a moment.)* Uh! *(Sits down and dials the telephone.)* Florence, honey, could you come on down for a moment. There's been a . . . little . . . accident . . . Quickly please. Uh! *(Loureen hangs up the phone. She gets a broom and a dust pan. She hesitantly approaches the pile of ashes. She gets down on her hands and knees and takes a closer look. A fatuous grin spreads across her face. She is startled by a sudden knock on the door. She slowly walks across the room like a possessed child. Loureen lets in Florence, her best friend and upstairs neighbor. Florence, also a housewife in her early thirties, wears a floral housecoat and a pair of over-sized slippers. Without acknowledgment Loureen proceeds to saunter back across the room.)*

FLORENCE: HEY!

LOUREEN: *(Pointing at the ashes:)* Uh! . . . *(She struggles to formulate words, which press at the inside of her mouth, not quite realized:)* Uh!

FLORENCE: You all right? What happened? *(Sniffs the air:)* Smells like you burned something? *(Stares at the huge pile of ashes:)* What the devil is that?

LOUREEN: *(Hushed:)* Samuel . . . It's Samuel, I think.

FLORENCE: What's he done now?

LOUREEN: It's him. It's him. *(Nods her head repeatedly.)*

FLORENCE: Chile, what's wrong with you? Did he finally drive you out of your mind? I knew something was going to happen sooner or later.

LOUREEN: Dial 911, Florence!

FLORENCE: Why? You're scaring me!

LOUREEN: Dial 911!

(Florence picks up the telephone and quickly dials.)

I think I killed him.

(Florence hangs up the telephone.)

FLORENCE: What?

LOUREEN: *(Whimpers:)* I killed him! I killed Samuel!

FLORENCE: Come again? . . . He's dead dead?

(Loureen wrings her hands and nods her head twice, mouthing "dead dead." Florence backs away.)

FLORENCE: No, stop it, I don't have time for this. I'm going back upstairs. You know how Samuel hates to find me here when he gets home. You're not going to get me this time. *(Louder:)* Y'all can have your little joke, I'm not part of it! *(A moment. She takes a hard look into Loureen's eyes; she squints:)* Did you really do it this time?

LOUREEN: *(Hushed:)* I don't know how or why it happened, it just did.

FLORENCE: Why are you whispering?

LOUREEN: I don't want to talk too loud — something else is liable to disappear.

FLORENCE: Where's his body?

LOUREEN: *(Points to the pile of ashes:)* There! . . .

FLORENCE: You burned him?

LOUREEN: I DON'T KNOW! *(Covers her mouth as if to muffle her words:)* I think so.

FLORENCE: Either you did or you didn't, what you mean you're talking murder, Loureen, not oven settings.

LOUREEN: You think I'm playing?

FLORENCE: How many times have I heard you talk about being rid of him. How many times have we sat at this table and laughed about the many ways we could do it and how many times have you done it? None.

LOUREEN: *(Lifting the spectacles:)* A pair of cheap spectacles, that's all that's left. And you know how much I hate these. You ever seen him without them, no! . . . He counted to four and disappeared. I swear to God!

FLORENCE: Don't bring the Lord into this just yet! Sit down now . . . What you got to sip on?

LOUREEN: I don't know whether to have a stiff shot of scotch or a glass of champagne.

(Florence takes a bottle of sherry out of the cupboard and pours them each a glass. Loureen downs hers, then holds out her glass for more.)

LOUREEN: He was.

FLORENCE: Take your time.

LOUREEN: Standing there.

FLORENCE: And?

LOUREEN: He exploded.

FLORENCE: Did that muthafucka hit you again?

LOUREEN: No . . . he exploded. Boom! Right in front of me. He was shouting like he does, being all colored, then he raised up that big crusty hand to hit me, and poof, he was gone . . . I barely got words out and I'm looking down at a pile of ash.

(Florence belts back her sherry. She wipes her forehead and pours them both another.)

FLORENCE: Chile, I'll give you this, in terms of color you've matched my husband Edgar, the story king. He came in at six Sunday morning, talking about he'd hit someone with his car, and had spent all night trying to outrun the police. I felt sorry for him. It turns out he was playing poker with his paycheck no less. You don't want to know how I found out . . . But I did.

LOUREEN: You think I'm lying?

FLORENCE: I certainly hope so, Loureen. For your sake and my heart's.

LOUREEN: Samuel always said if I raised my voice something horrible would happen. And it did. I'm a witch . . . the devil spawn!

FLORENCE: You've been watching too much television.

LOUREEN: Never seen anything like this on television. Wish I had, then I'd know what to do . . . There's no question, I'm a witch. *(Looks at her hands with disgust.)*

FLORENCE: Chile, don't tell me you've been messing with them mojo women again? What did I tell ya.

(Loureen, agitated, stands and sits back down.)

LOUREEN: He's not coming back. Oh no, how could he? It would be a miracle! Two in one day . . . I could be canonized. Worse yet, he could be . . . All that needs to happen is for my palms to bleed and I'll be eternally remembered as Saint Loureen, the patron of battered wives. Women from across the country will make pilgrimages to me, laying pies and pot roast at my feet and asking the good saint to make their husbands turn to dust. How often does a man like Samuel get damned to hell, and go?

(She breaks down. Florence moves to console her friend, then realizes that Loureen is actually laughing hysterically.)

FLORENCE: You smoking crack?

LOUREEN: Do I look like I am?

FLORENCE: Hell, I've seen old biddies creeping out of crack houses, talking about they were doing church work.

LOUREEN: Florence, please be helpful. I'm very close to the edge. . . . I don't know what to do next! Do I sweep him up? Do I call the police?

. . .

I should be mourning, I should be praying, I should be thinking of the burial, but all that keeps popping into my mind is what will I wear on television when I share my horrible and wonderful story with a studio audience . . . *(Whimpers:)* He's made me a killer, Florence, and you remember what a gentle child I was. *(Whispers:)* I'm a killer, I'm a killer, I'm a killer.

END OF SCENE

The Radiant Abyss
Angus MacLachlan

Dramatic
Erin, forty
Ina, early twenties

Erin runs a business in a local strip mall which she believes is threatened when a nutty religious group moves in next door. She hopes to manipulate Ina into helping her get rid of them.

ERIN: *(Whispered tenderly.)* Hello little fishy. Good morning . . . You're not a moron, are you. *(Uncharacteristically still, she takes a moment or two to watch the fish.)* Imagine living in a world where no one feeds you . . . Or watches out for you. And instead of clean water you're suffocating from filth . . . *(Pause. Takes a breath. She puts some more fish food in — then stops.)* Shit. Did I already do that? . . . Sorry. *(She gives a short guffaw.)* Well, we could all end up in the toilet, couldn't we? *(Then she resumes her pace. She gradually becomes aware of a light tapping at the back door. She looks at the clock, frowns, and heads to the hall.)* Peaches? . . . *(She exits to open the door. Offstage.)* Oh! . . . Are you all right? . . . Well — *(She enters.)* All alone? *(A strikingly sallow exhausted Ina enters wheeling her ten-speed bike, and quickly, subtly, scans the room — no Steve Enloe. She is dressed in her Kinko's khakis, white shirt, and blue apron, and wearing a backpack. She looks like she's been through the wringer, and the end of the line came a few hours earlier. Now she's barely holding it together — mostly from sheer will. Fragile.)*

INA: Could, can I bring this in here?

ERIN: Sure. Just — *(Ina leans her bike up in the back hallway. Erin is a bit thrown by her, and seems puzzled — almost wary, or even slightly vulnerable to Ina's presence.)* What happened? Uh — Where's Steve Enloe, is he coming? How did it go? What happened? What did he do? Oh — *(She looks at the time.)* Shoot — wait — Excuse me just one second. I've got a business to run. And we open in half an hour . . . *(Erin sits at the computer and types fast.)* Let me just get this, and these boxes for pick-up before . . . *(Without asking, Ina collapses in a chair near the desk and immediately gets a Hardees bag of french fries out of her backpack and starts to nibble. She giggles some.)*

INA: . . . And I'm not sick anymore.

ERIN: *(Glances at her.)* Good.

INA: Yeah. This morning.

ERIN: Hm . . . You just woke up and you weren't nauseous? I've heard that happens sometimes.

INA: You want some?

ERIN: No, thank you.

INA: So, like, I went through the drive-thru on my bike. Ever done that? . . . It just hits me funny . . . I guess I'm kind of punchy, 'cause I never went to sleep — So, I didn't "just wake up," but around about, maybe 5:37 I felt like I wasn't going to throw up anymore. And this morning I wanted fries. *(She eats.)* And I tried, but I couldn't. Sleeping . . . Your home phone is unlisted? Is that 'cause of business? So your tenants can't harass you or anything?

ERIN: — You looked me up?

INA: Or is it just 'cause of . . . bitchiness? *(Smiles.)* . . . Huh? *(Erin stops typing and looks at her, puzzled. She bites her tongue. Unsure how to react to her oddness, she glances at the time, gets up and goes to the boxes, moving them towards the back door.)*

ERIN: Sorry, I have to get these ready. *(Ina eats, doesn't watch her. Erin observes her while she works. Pause.)* Everything went OK, though, right?

INA: Was he with you last night? *(This stops Erin completely. She straightens, turns, and looks at her.)*

ERIN: What?

INA: Tell me. *(Erin moves slowly towards her a bit, wary.)*

ERIN: . . . What's going on, Ina?

INA: Well. Erin. You're asking the wrong person. So, um, you tell me.

ERIN: Uh . . . Did he not come home? . . . I don't know where he was. He wasn't with me. *(Ina eats.)* Why . . . would he be? . . . When did you last see him?

INA: Here. Yesterday afternoon.

ERIN: What? — Wait — Did you go do the — did you go last night?

INA: Of course.

ERIN: Did Steve Enloe? . . . Do you know?

INA: I haven't seen him since yesterday afternoon. *(Erin tries to figure this out.)*

. . .

ERIN: I was wondering if I could see if he got in next door — if I could tell — but —

INA: Yeah, I tried that earlier — Zilch.

ERIN: — Have you been riding around on your bike all night?

INA: Um. Some. Yeah. I got to go to Kinko's soon. I'm late now. It was a nice night. I mean, the weather. And it was quiet. Do you have a bike? *(Thinking, Erin grabs her cell and presses speed dial.)*

ERIN: You should go home and get some sleep.

INA: *(Mouth full.)* You want some?

ERIN: *(On the phone. Charming.)* Good morning, John, how are you? — Are you still in bed? *(She laughs huskily.)* Oops. I'm sorry. *(Whispers.)* Tell Caroline I'm sorry — But, goodness, it's close to 8:00. Didn't you leave *me* a message — ? Ohhh. Then you went back to bed? *(Laughs.)* What a life you have, Deputy-Sheriff. Power *is* delicious, isn't it? *(Laughs.)* So, tell me about our little lovebirds, the Santiagos. Un-huh. Did they do any damage? *(She pours Ina some coffee. Ina takes it, but doesn't sip.)* So you — or — somebody — not you, since you don't roll out of bed till the crack of noon — but, somebody will be patrolling today? *(Smiles.)* Oh, I feel safer. *(Laughs.)* . . . Say — has anyone seen the Santiagos around my office? . . . Well, we have security till two for the whole strip mall, you know, but I've heard nothing. Uh-huh . . . You either. No reports . . . No vandalism. Good . . . Well, keep an eye peeled. *(Laughs.)* I know you will. Sure. Good. Umn. *(Whispers.)* Bye to Caroline. Bye. *(Hangs up.)* Nothing's been reported.

INA: You have a lot of friends. *(Erin looks at her, getting her inference.)*

ERIN: Hell. That moron knows nothing.

INA: Do you have milk? I'm sort of off coffee these days.

ERIN: Oh. Yeah, I think so.

INA: Thanks . . . I miss coffee. *(Erin gets milk from the fridge and pours some in a mug and hands it to her.)*

ERIN: I wasn't thinking. *(Ina hands her back the coffee, then gets another hot apple pie from her backpack.)*

INA: . . . I'm ravenous. I haven't been in such a long time, you know? Have you ever been pregnant? *(Erin looks at her. The question hangs in the air. Erin takes a breath.)* It's no fun. If you ask me. But, that's just me. This friend of a friend of mine — Amy? — she loved it. The whole time. But I think it's kind of sucky so far. But we'll see. It's still early on. Maybe I'm just getting to the good part. Do they ever come this early?

ERIN: Who?

INA: Next door. Do they hang around in the daytime?

ERIN: Not quite this early.

INA: Then we wait, I guess, to find out the truth . . . Or, till somebody turns up . . . I want him to tell me to my face, I guess. What he did. Or something. *(Ina turns to Erin. Erin looks at her.)*

ERIN: Well, I have no idea where he is this morning. Really. *(Ina stares at her, then finishes the pie and wipes her mouth.)*

INA: He's gone, I think.

ERIN: Huh? What?

INA: Maybe we'll get lucky and he's dead.

ERIN: What makes you say that? *(Ina stops, overcome suddenly, in exhausted giggling. She stops herself and pulls it together.)*

INA: . . . God knows. *(She laughs again. Concerned, Erin sits near Ina.)*

ERIN: I. OK. Tell me exactly what happened with you last night.

INA: At the church? I got there early, like 7:43, and near the end I hid in the bathroom, and I left the side door unlocked, and then I rode my bike home.

ERIN: And he never showed up and he never called?

INA: Nope.

ERIN: Has he ever left you before?

INA: — Didn't your husband leave you?

ERIN: No. I fled.

INA: Hm.

ERIN: Don't worry. He'll turn up. He always does. Like a dirty penny.

INA: Aren't you sweet.

ERIN: Ina —

INA: I mean it. Thanks for the milk. I can't finish it all. It's just a little bit sour. I think it's past its due date. *(Pause.)*

ERIN: . . . You want to tell me about the service? *(Ina starts to giggle.)*

INA: Just a minute.

ERIN: What? *(Erin sits with her.)*

INA: I'm so tired. *(Ina gathers herself again. Without rancor.)* I just want to say one thing first. Fuck you, Erin. I don't mean that disrespectful, I just mean it. *(Ina looks at Erin directly.)*

ERIN: OK.

INA: You knew what I was getting into. It was all your idea. I mean, he didn't think up that plan, did he? For me to go there.

ERIN: No.

INA: Just to mock me? 'Cause I don't believe in God?

ERIN: No. What do you mean? —

INA: To be cruel?

ERIN: — I thought we needed some help . . . *No.*

INA: You want to know what it was like? OK. Well, it was long. And they had incense. And the women had, like . . . oppressive clothes. But, truth be told — when I first got there . . . um . . .

ERIN: Did they stop you at the door?

INA: Nah, I walked right in, and this woman with this thing on her head gave me a hug right off the bat. And then this old man. And when he hugged me he called me his daughter and held me really close.

ERIN: God. Did he smell bad too?

INA: It was kind of — you now — uh . . .

ERIN: I know. They're —

INA: . . . I kind of liked it.

ERIN: What?

INA: Yeah. At first. He held me — not weird, you know — sweet. And there wasn't any snakes. Or any talk about violence. They were nice. *(A beat.)*

ERIN: Right. With that smile plastered on their faces. They're all that way till you open your mouth, and question their —

INA: Nothing really bothered me till they got us to sit down and the men set up front and all the women had to sit in the back.

ERIN: Of course.

INA: And they started talking God. Changing Your Life, and His Power, and Love, and, I thought — yuck, get me out of here, this is making me sick — but then we all held hands. All the women . . . And that was nice. Holding hands. And then everybody started to sing, and it got real hot with all those people crammed in there. And the incense. And that made me sort of light-headed, you know? And then they *really* got into it. And it got crazy.

ERIN: What did they say? Is that when it came out? The fanatical, extremist —

INA: I started to feel kind of woozy, you know, and just as I was about to run find a bathroom this lady beside me dropped to the floor — right there in front of me — shaking and moaning —

ERIN: Oh, uhn-huh . . .

INA: And then more women started dropping like flies. Just flopping around. And these men at the front began screaming about The Power . . . It's hard to describe.

ERIN: Oh, no, I know exactly what you mean —

INA: Cause when you're in the middle of it?

ERIN: Yeah?

INA: You couldn't not feel something. Electric. Really. I felt it. This — power — was there. All around me. These men chanting, and swaying. The women writhing. And screaming "In the name of God. In the name of God." It just makes me so . . . so . . . sick.

ERIN: I'm sure.

INA: And . . . so . . . pissed —

ERIN: I know! When they start with their —

INA: At you.

ERIN: — At me?

INA: Because I thought we were doing something. Together. But I get your little joke, now. You and Steve Enloe. You don't care what they're up to. You just wanted to make sport, —

ERIN: No — What? — I —

INA: *(Continuing over Erin's line.)* — and laugh at me. 'Cause of my beliefs.

ERIN: No! No — I want to stop them —

INA: Just SHUT UP. I get it! Stop playing with me. Like you do. With him. *(A beat.)*

INA: WHERE IS HE?!

ERIN: — Ina —

INA: You know what it was like? I, I, I felt like I was on the edge of this — just staring down into — like when you look over a mountain and you want to jump. Into something bottomless. And exciting. I had to, to really fight, you know, to pull myself back. From getting sucked . . . Those men — this Passion — so worked up. But in control. And those women . . . Those women . . . Falling for it . . . Falling . . . 'Cause it felt like . . . it felt . . . So real . . . so — *(A beat.)* . . . But I *know.* It's *not.* It's nothing but lies. They're lost in nothing. They're lying to themselves. Flinging themselves around like that . . . I guess they're just, you know — they're buying into it 'cause they want it so much. You know?

ERIN: But — Ina — that's not what we object to. It's the — it's that they're covering up their real motivation. It's the *lie* —

INA: And it's really really dangerous, if you ask me —

ERIN: It *is* dangerous — because they don't want to do good, they want to hurt other people. Anyone who doesn't believe in —

INA: — To believe in a lie that big. I think. And everything that goes with it. 'Cause you could be made to do anything — you don't even know. With that much desperation? And I was glad at the time 'cause I thought, you know — that we were gonna do something about it.

ERIN: I do! I want to —

INA: That Steve Enloe was going to do something later to them. Mess things up. I thought we were on a mission. 'Cause — man — that place is FUCKED UP. These people are *fucked up!* — But when I came home, and he never showed, I pretty much figured it out. Ha ha. The joke's on me.

ERIN: *(Softly.)* Wait a minute, wait a minute — you're —

INA: You really are a bitch.

ERIN: I'm — but that . . . "church" . . . I — I really don't believe that you got the whole point. Maybe you missed something when you were hiding in the bathroom. Because we've heard countless —

INA: You just did it to hurt me 'cause I'm his real girlfriend. *(Erin stops a moment, arrested.)*

ERIN: . . . I wouldn't do that.

INA: And that's so stupid. Especially if — So, tell me the truth, for once — *please.* He *really* didn't spend the night with you?

ERIN: Why would he?

INA: *Please.*

ERIN: *NO.* No. He didn't.

INA: Really?

ERIN: I'm telling you the truth.

INA: Hm. OK . . .

ERIN: Oh. God, Ina. OK — Steve Enloe and I — It's nothing. It's —

INA: Some joke.

ERIN: It's an old . . . habit. It's meaningless — It's not worth you getting —

INA: Like I care? When I know he's fucking someone else . . .

ERIN: No no no. Listen — I —

INA: Yeah, this high school chick, Allison, who works at Kinko's with me. *(Pause.)* She says she's sixteen but she's not even. *(Pause.)* And if he really wasn't with you last night, then I'm sure that's where he was. 'Cause, she's in this band and she's got this ass. And Steve Enloe loves butterbeans. *(A beat.)*

ERIN: What?

INA: Yeah. So. fuck you too, huh . . . I guess we both know who we're dealing with . . . *(Pause.)* You don't even know why you do what you do, do you? *(Ina becomes very quiet, very sad.)* But I do . . . I think. *(Pause. Ina gets up.)* I'm sorry, I have to pee, now. Excuse me. *(She exits. The phone on the desk rings.)*

ERIN: *(On phone.)* Skidmore Property . . . This is not the Driver's License Bureau! *(She slams it down. Erin stalks about the room, shaking her head, pulling her hair. She stops at the fishbowl for a second, and looks at it. Her anger turns — something hurt, vulnerable, rising.)*

INA: *(Offstage.)* You're out of paper! Do you have any more? *(Erin looks to the bathroom. Then she rummages through a cabinet and takes a roll offstage.)*

ERIN: *(Offstage.)* Sorry about that. It's Miss Chitty's job.

INA: *(Offstage.)* Thanks . . . Are you OK?

ERIN: *(Offstage.)* Me? *(A flush is heard. After a moment Erin enters with Ina — upset, beginning to shatter a bit. Erin, unfamiliar how to deal with someone so vulnerable, stands near her, awkwardly. Her hand hovers as if to touch Ina's shoulder, but she doesn't. Ina wipes her nose and tries to pull out of it.)*

INA: Sometimes I just want to kill him.

ERIN: He's not even worth it.

INA: — Do you have any doughnuts?

ERIN: What are you going to do now, honey?

INA: I'm still hungry. *(Erin looks at her, directly.)*

ERIN: I think you should get out.

INA: You want me to leave . . . ?

ERIN: I mean it. Can you? *(Pause.)* You're not an idiot, like the — I've seen all these girls over these years, and — really— it is a goddamn mystery to me how he does it. What is it with him?

INA: Well, he's, uh . . . He can be sweet.

ERIN: All I can say is, I pray to God he *did* leave you. That would be the easiest thing.

INA: That's not nice.

ERIN: She's only *fifteen?* And already mixed up with that prick? Jesus Christ.

INA: I know it's really bad — But, what are you going to do.,

ERIN: Come on! Are you blind?! You're NOT STUPID. You're not like the others! All of the idiots.

INA: OK, don't. Erin —

ERIN: And I'm just as bad! That's what's so — GOD ALMIGHTY! —

INA: Stop yelling. Please. Or.

ERIN: — INFURIATING!!!

INA: OK, I'll just go, OK? *(Ina starts to gather her things to go.)*

ERIN: — I'M SUCH A GOD DAMN *MORON*. He's not even that good a fuck!

INA: — Bye —

ERIN: Stop it! Ina! *(Ina stops.)*

INA: What? *(A beat.)*

ERIN: Do something decisive. Now. Whatever it takes.

INA: I'm going to do something. I want to talk to him. I want to hear what . . . And, you know, *I* know that he doesn't mean to be bad.

ERIN: That's what's so dangerous. *(She motions to her center. Her heart.)* He's evil!

INA: No, he's not. — He's just — He's Steve Enloe. And we're — see — He's — it's different with us, 'cause he and I — we're going to be . . .

ERIN: That's what I mean! Great day in the morning! *(She laughs a snort.)* If there *is* a God he *won't* come back.

INA: But he, he might — like you said.

ERIN: Honey, you don't have to live like this — believe me! I know what I'm talking about.

INA: No — I — he's, he's not all bad. And he cares about me — I think. *(Beat.)*

ERIN: What makes you think that?

INA: I feel it.

ERIN: Ohh darlin'. Oh darlin'. If you don't stop lying to yourself — later on, it's going to — I mean literally — kill you . . . Listen to me. You know, I was up all night too. *(She takes a step closer.)* If you can't find the strength to do it for yourself, think about . . . Look at what's right in front of your nose. What's the future with Steve Enloe going to be? . . . You've got to put an end to it. One way or another. This is the time.

INA: . . . What, what do you mean? *(A beat.)*

ERIN: What do you want?

INA: Oh God . . .

ERIN: You got to make a choice.

INA: . . . Like . . . ?

ERIN: Something bold, whatever it takes. You've got a brain . . . Think hard . . . Take responsibility. *(A beat.)*

INA: Then what?

ERIN: Go back to your family.

INA: I can't.

ERIN: Or to some friend, some — somebody. Anybody! It's just — It's your *own* life. LET IT MEAN SOMETHING!

INA: *(Tremulous.)* But . . . this is my family now. *(Pause.)*

ERIN: Oh, hon. *(Erin moves to her. She reaches out and caresses Ina's face. Sadly. Lovingly. Ina lets her. Erin shakes her head, and holds Ina's face. A tender, multi-faceted exchange/moment between them.)*

END OF SCENE

Secretary of Shake

Eisa Davis

Dramatic

25 and 36 (these are their ages)

25 and 36 are two actresses waiting to audition for a reality TV show.

(a warehouse. a beautiful woman dressed in a velour sweatsuit (36) walks in and sits on a chair next to another woman, who wears a terry cloth sweat-suit (25). there is a full-length mirror on the wall between them. they wait.)

25: you going in first?

36: my audition was for 2. you?

25: 215. must be running behind.
are they taking people according to appointment time or sign-in time?

36: I don't know. but you signed in first, you can go.

25: no, you were at 2. you go.

36: it doesn't matter. whatever. they'll call us.
(a silence.)

25: it's kinda weird to be auditioning for a reality show.

36: why? they already got cameras on us all the time. might as well get paid for it.
this place is way out in the boonies, though. I want reimbursement for my mileage.

25: yeah, well they have to be top secret about it. did you go through that security check?

36: oh mama. and the background check?

25: mine was pretty easy, only 2 weeks long.

36: huh.

25: how long was yours?

36: something like that.
(a silence, 36 begins to remove her sweats, revealing silver or gold lamé hot pants. she begins to stretch. 25 takes off her sweats as well, and is dressed in an equally erotic outfit.)

25: so what did you major in in school?

36: I was organic chemistry with a concentration in biological weaponry.

25: that's perfect. I was international relations, focusing on Korean/South Asian/Middle Eastern nuclear proliferation, with a minor in German history. any field work in intelligence?

36: if I had it I couldn't tell you.

25: diplomacy?

36: what's this we're doing right now?

25: when did you start dancing?

36: question is when will I stop?

25: you've done so many videos. this is strange to say but it's even stranger if I don't — I've been watching your work for years and you're my idol.

36: thank you.

25: and archrival. it always comes down to me and you when they're casting the main ho.

36: I've caught your work too. I always know when a move is out of date once you do it.

25: actually, I'd call myself an unsung originator. remember the Sammy Say So shoot?

36: barely. I was in the hot tub. favor for a friend.

25: I was working Sammy out with this —

(25 does moves.)

36: oh I remember that one.

25: and this —

(another move.)

36: girl, nuh uh.

25: and then —

(the move de move.)

36: yeah that was the bomb and the — isn't there a hair flip at the end?

25: exactly. I made up the whole routine and then they gave it to this other ho with a blond weave.

36: if you have blond hair, that's hotter, people will always choose you to be the main ho. it's just business and we're in it.

25: but your weave is red.

36: it's to set me apart.

25: so they gave the blond bitch my moves which *everyone* bit after that. put her in every men's magazine swimsuit issue. and they put *me* in the hot tub. that's where I met you.

36: I don't remember.

25: we were kissing. in the hot tub? they wanted some girl-on-girl so it would look hot.

36: that was you? they have me kissing every ho these days.

25: I couldn't believe it was you, who I looked up to — I mean all the strippers and drag queens bite your style.

36: well. I just know what gets em started that's all. show me what you're going to do in there, I'll give you some pointers.

25: really?

36: I told you — diplomacy is key.

(25 stands up and does a few moves.)

25: I'm going to do my new shit, a style nobody has seen —

36: nice, that was a nice one —

25: then I'll just tweak em out with something at the end, just something they won't expect, like —

(25 pulls open her top and flashes her nipple.)

36: *why did you do that?*

25: because — I don't know — it was funny. an ironic reference.

36: you can't be ironic in this job.

25: it was a joke!

36: don't be smart! they don't want smart!

25: but I am!

36: then what was your smarty pants joke *for?*

25: I don't know, it was an impulse. I was making a comment. and my body is beautiful, what's wrong with showing it?

36: *(an oath to the sky.)* in the name of Katherine Dunham, Alvin Ailey, and Savion Glover, let me save this child. *(to 25.)* they don't want that. the nipple? you think that's funny? no. it's too real. makes em start thinking about their nanny and slavery. you don't want reality on a reality show! I'm serious as a heart attack. now listen to me — are you listening? you must *tease.* don't *ever* give up the nipple! keep it covered. *that's* hardcore. *that's* the key to diplomacy. *that's* your big stick. the nipple is what they have to get on their knees and beg for.

(36 suddenly notices a hidden camera filming them.)

36: *(to camera.)* yes?

(no answer. she stands up and shakes her hair out, utilizing every moment to determine the best strategy to use.)

36: you want to know why I want to be a back up dancer to the Secretary of State? I need stability 'cause them damn videos don't pay rent —

(25 overlaps 36's lines as they try to upstage each other for the camera.)

25: well, you get to travel —

36: can you see me at the damn post office —

25: meeting the people who run the planet would be really interesting —

36: *(to 25.)* let's take this one at a time. you first. tell him why you want to be on *Secretary of Shake. (under her breath.)* and *don't* be smart!

25: I think — I think that — life is too separated. um — people get mad when certain things or people come together that they think should stay apart, but everything needs everything else, like night needs day to feel special, the moon needs the sun to look cool, and the Secretary of State should have back up dancers because — it's more fun and there would be less war.

36: now me. look. I'm never back up, I am always the main ho. I am the principal dancer, the prime mover — that's an anatomical term I like to use on suckers like you. but let me tell you something. we need some change. we've got to have some dance ambassadors to set things straight cross this world. and let me say, if I could tour with the Secretary of State — *this* Secretary of State who rocks the mic like she do, flipping facts like flapjacks, this ho who is so gangsta she don't even have meetings 'cause she ain't interested in what anyone else have to say, I mean somebody who rolls like that needs some back up dancers. like fully. like now. like it's a crime she been doin her geopolitical thing without us. if I taught her some moves, we could actually get somewhere. think about it. my girl don't even know where her body is! once she get out of her head tryin to prove she's smarter than everybody, I could teach her a lot about herself. *and* I know French.

(to 25.) dance.

(25 starts to move.)

25: like this?

36: perfect.

(36 begins to move too. the women dance in silence. and lights fade . . .)

END OF SCENE

The Spirit is Willing
Nicole Quinn

Dramatic
Barbara and Johanna, forties to fifties

Barbara dated Johanna in high school, only her name was John then and he was on his way to law school. As a skeptical reporter at a New Age Expo, Barbara must face some unvarnished truths about herself.

(Barbara Manning, a comely, upscale, reporter in her middle years, talks into a mini tape recorder.)

BARBARA: . . . Everything from EST to witchcraft. There's even an expert on "UFO abduction phenomenon." One holdover from the sixties, a local Swami, who once made his living writing for "Hustler", now offers workshops in "Sex as a Doorway to Divinity." . . .

(Johanna, a handsome woman of about Barbara's age, moves out of the center booth.)

JOHANNA: Barbara?

BARBARA: *(Turns in confusion.)* Yes?

JOHANNA: *(Menacing:)* I know your past.

BARBARA: *(Startled:)* Excuse me?

(Johanna crosses to her.)

JOHANNA: It's John Biddle . . . Johanna now, Muncie Indiana? You look fabulous. Just eyes or whole face? How's your mother?

BARBARA: *(Confused:)* Johanna Biddle? It sounds familiar.

JOHANNA: John. We went out twice, senior year. Once for fun and once so you could mock me in front of the entire class. Remember?

BARBARA: *(Recognition dawns.)* Not "little Biddle"?

JOHANNA: Not anymore. I had it snipped.

BARBARA: My God!

JOHANNA: I thought I was, until you dashed my dreams. Just as well, really. The experience prepared me for the rest of the size queens who tip the scales at meat over motion. *(She indicates the recorder.)* Could you turn that off? I'm not anxious to become one of the curios you collect on this hunting expedition.

(Barbara clicks off the recorder.)

JOHANNA: So, tell me, Barbara, are you still a self-centered bitch?

BARBARA: Do I detect a note of bitterness?

JOHANNA: Take it as a compliment, sweetie. Some of us actually admired you for it. Even in grammar school, you were the only one who got to see foreskins without having to bare any skin yourself.

BARBARA: You remember more about me than I do.

JOHANNA: Because I studied you. It must have been very lonely being Barbara.

BARBARA: I see you've taken a degree in amateur psychology.

JOHANNA: Paranormal psychology actually.

BARBARA: You're joking.

JOHANNA: No, I'm not.

BARBARA: But I heard that you became a lawyer.

JOHANNA: So I did.

BARBARA: Do you practice?

JOHANNA: Only numerology and tarot.

BARBARA: Male lawyer turned female gypsy. What a story.

JOHANNA: A little too "true confessions" even for you, dear.

BARBARA: Did you have any children?

JOHANNA: Three. Two girls and a boy.

BARBARA: And are you their father or mother?

JOHANNA: Father. Surgical technology hasn't come that far yet.

BARBARA: So, you were gay.

JOHANNA: No, I was a woman trapped in a man's body. Now I'm gay.

BARBARA: *(Shocked:)* You changed your sex to become a lesbian?

JOHANNA: I changed my sex to become a woman. Consequently, men have never turned me on.

BARBARA: Oh . . .

(Barbara backs away involuntarily.)

JOHANNA: Don't worry, dear, you're no longer my type. Too socially correct, too waspy, too mean. Tell me, is your husband still fucking the starlet?

BARBARA: *(Direct hit.)* I see I should have attended some of those high school reunions. Muncie's not as dull as it used to be. What else do you divine in my aura?

JOHANNA: I needn't divine anything about you. I follow your byline, dear. And since that charming bit of exhibitionism on "Lifestyles of the Rich and Famous," your daily existence has become an open tabloid. Why are you here, Barbara? To ridicule and humiliate?

BARBARA: To inform.

JOHANNA: Meditation and past life regression doesn't seem quite your beat.

BARBARA: I'm curious.

JOHANNA: Anxious to find out how many peons you had beheaded, or the acreage of your plantation?

BARBARA: *(Hostile:)* Something like that.

JOHANNA: That was judgmental of me, wasn't it? I do apologize. I'm operating on out of date information. For all I know you might be very enlightened.

(Johanna bursts out laughing.)

BARBARA: Now what?

JOHANNA: I was trying to imagine you with a titanium pyramid on your head.

BARBARA: Do you honestly believe in any of this New Age hype?

JOHANNA: If you sift through enough crap, you might find a few genuine spiritualists here.

BARBARA: And how does one tell the real from the fake?

JOHANNA: Basic instinct. And I don't mean dykes with ice picks. But then I don't suppose your exposé has room to embrace simple truths.

BARBARA: Such as?

JOHANNA: Ordinary people living plain and exemplary lives amidst chaos and confusion. Using their gifts, with little fanfare, for the well being of others.

BARBARA: So this iconographic display is not a parody of itself, and these gurus are not gold digging merchants masquerading as Messiahs?

JOHANNA: That's not what I mean at all. There are definitely those here who enlighten their pockets as they hawk the new age version of the dashboard Jesus. But behind all the acting and the artifice, the seeming charade of it all, there are also those who see things, terrifying things unappeased and dangerous, lurking in the dark. And if you seek with unveiled eyes, Barbara, you just might see those angels.

BARBARA: Tell me, John, do you see them?

JOHANNA: Everyday. Just as one sees God. With the mind and the heart.

END OF SCENE

They're Just Like Us
Boo Killebrew

Dramatic
Ann and Jen, twenties

Ann and Jen are friends but there is obviously much competition between them. Ann has just returned from Africa after adopting a child. Jen has been in and out of rehab for an eating disorder and drug problem.

(Ann walks in. Jen runs in after her.)
JEN: Oh my God!
ANN: Oh my God, hey!
JEN: Wow, welcome back.
ANN: Thanks.
JEN: I was calling your name back there.
ANN: Oh.
JEN: When did you get back?
ANN: Oh, like a month ago.
JEN: Wow, I can't believe that. Where you been hiding?
ANN: Well, I'm pretty busy these days. With the baby.
JEN: Oh my God! How's the baby?
ANN: Good, really good.
JEN: I'm so sorry, I totally forgot that you have a baby now!
ANN: Yeah, from Africa.
JEN: Oh my God! How's the African baby?
ANN: Great, really great.
JEN: Girl or boy?
ANN: You didn't hear?
JEN: No.
ANN: It's a girl.
JEN: What did you name her?
ANN: You didn't hear about any of this?

JEN: Well, a lot has been going on, Ann. I knew you were adopting an African baby, but I didn't hear any details.

ANN: You didn't get the christening FaxBlast?

JEN: I'm not getting anyone's FaxBlasts these days.

ANN: I gave her an African name.

JEN: How sweet!

ANN: Her name is —

JEN: — Is she so cute?

ANN: Yes, she's wonderful.

JEN: Do you feel weird?

ANN: A little.

JEN: I felt really weird after I was hospitalized for exhaustion.

ANN: You were hospitalized for exhaustion?

JEN: Yeah, I guess you missed that.

ANN: Yeah, I was probably in Africa adopting my baby at that time.

JEN: I'm okay now, please don't worry about me. I just want everyone to forget about that and the rehab.

ANN: Rehab?

JEN: Yes, Ann, but please don't worry. I'm fine now.

ANN: Okay.

JEN: I'm fine.

ANN: Okay.

JEN: Really.

ANN: Okay.

(Pause.)

ANN: Have you seen Gene and Frank lately?

JEN: Oh yeah, I saw them at Marty's big Outer Space Birthday Party.

ANN: Marty the retard?

JEN: He's not retarded, Ann. He's slow.

ANN: Oh.

JEN: He's a beautiful soul.

ANN: Oh.

JEN: His party was slammin'. The Biz, Beth Foster —

ANN: Neither Frank nor Gene has called me since I've been back from Africa.

JEN: You know how it is, everyone is so busy these days, Ann.

ANN: I know, I'm busy too, but you would think that they at least would have called or texted.

JEN: Have you tried calling them?

ANN: Yes, but every time I call either of them it says their number has been changed.

JEN: Oh yeah, you weren't here for that.

ANN: What happened?

JEN: Frank's crazy ex-boyfriend, Mickey — have you seen "Divine Justice" lately?

ANN: I've been in Africa.

(Jen looks at her blankly.)

ANN: No, I haven't seen "Divine Justice" lately.

JEN: Frank's ex-boyfriend Mickey is now an actor on that show, you know the one with dark skin and curly brown hair?

ANN: I don't know.

JEN: Anyway, Mickey was calling Frank all the time, begging for him to take him back, so Frank had to change his number. Gene said he had to change his number, but wouldn't tell anyone why.

ANN: Really? Is Gene still a mystery?

JEN: I think Gene will always be a mystery.

ANN: Yeah.

JEN: But look, we should all get together and have a drink or something. You can bring your baby.

ANN: I don't really know if a bar is the best place for me to bring —

JEN: — Brunch! We'll do a brunch!

ANN: Okay.

JEN: When I see Gene and Frank online tonight we'll set the whole thing up.

ANN: Well, if you see Gene and Frank online, could you please tell them to call, text, or email me. I'd really like to talk to them.

JEN: Of course.

ANN: I'll call you.

JEN: Just text! This is my new number.

ANN: Okay.

JEN: Ann —

ANN: Yeah?

(A soft moment.)

JEN: Please do not give it out.

ANN: Okay.

JEN: It was really great to see you.

ANN: You too, I'm really sorry to hear that you were in the hospital and in rehab.

JEN: Thank you. Try not to talk about it with anyone, okay?

ANN: I really just talk to my African baby these days.

JEN: Well, don't tell your baby, okay?

ANN: Okay. I'll call you!

JEN: Just text! It's easier. Bye!

ANN: Bye!

END OF SCENE

Rights and Permissions

All That I Will Ever Be. © 2007 by Alan Ball. Reprinted by permission of Seth Glewen, The Gersh Agency, 41 Madison Ave., New York, NY 10010. The entire text has been published by Dramatists Play Service, 440 Park Ave. S., New York, NY 10016. 212-MU3-8960 (www.dramatists.com), who also handle performance rights.

All This Intimacy. © 2006 by Rajiv Joseph. Reprinted by permission of Seth Glewen, The Gersh Agency, 41 Madison Ave., New York, NY 10010. The entire text has been published by Samuel French, Inc., 45 W. 25th St., New York, NY 10010. 212-206-8990. (www.samuelfrench.com), who also handle performance rights.

Asylum. © 2006 by Keith Aisner. All rights reserved. Reprinted by permission of Playscripts, Inc. To purchase acting editions of this play, or to obtain stock or amateur performance rights, you must contact Playscripts, Inc. (Website: www.playscripts.com) (E-mail: info@playscripts.com). Phone 866-NEW-PLAY (866-639-7529).

BFF. © 2007 by Anna Ziegler. Reprinted by permission of Peregrine Whittlesey, 279 Central Park W. #23, New York, NY 10024. 212-787-1802 (pwwagy@aol.com), who also handles performance rights. Contact Peregrine Whittlesey for further information.

Bhutan. © 2007 by Daisy Foote. Reprinted by permission of Beth Blickers, Abrams Artists Agency, 275 7th Ave., New York, NY 10001. The entire text has been published by Dramatists Play Service, 440 Park Ave. S., New York, NY 10016. 212-MU3-8960 (www.dramatists.com), who also handle performance rights.

Blur. © 2006 by Melanie Marnich. All rights reserved. Reprinted by permission of Playscripts, Inc. To purchase acting editions of this play, or to obtain stock or amateur performance rights, you must contact Playscripts, Inc. (Website: www.playscripts.com) (E-mail: info@playscripts.com). Phone: 866-NEW-PLAY (866-639-7529).

Bye, Bye, Margarita. © 2006 by Gavin Lawrence. All rights reserved. Reprinted by permission of Playscripts, Inc. To purchase acting editions of this play, or to obtain stock or amateur performance rights, you must contact Playscripts, Inc. (Website: www.playscripts.com) (E-mail: info@playscripts.com). Phone: 866-NEW-PLAY (866-639-7529).

Check Please, Take Two. © 2006 by Jonathan Rand. All rights reserved. Reprinted by permission of Playscripts, Inc. To purchase acting editions of this play, or to obtain stock or amateur performance rights, you must contact Playscripts, Inc. (Website: www.playscripts.com) (E-mail: info@playscripts.com). Phone: 866-NEW-PLAY (866-639-7529).

County Line. © 2006 by Christina Hamm. All rights reserved. Reprinted by permission of Playscripts, Inc. To purchase acting editions of this play, or to obtain stock or amateur performance rights, you must contact Playscripts, Inc. (Website: www.playscripts.com) (E-mail: info@playscripts.com). Phone: 866-NEW-PLAY (866-639-7529).

Dark Play; or, Stories for Boys. © 2006 by Carlos Murillo. Reprinted by permission of Antje Oegel, Bret Adams, Ltd., 448 W. 44th St., New York, NY 10036. For inquiries concerning all rights, contact: Bruce Ostler, Bret Adams Ltd., 448 West 44th Street, New York, NY 10036

The Dead Guy. © 2006 by Eric Coble. Reprinted by permission of Val Day, William Morris Agency, 1325 Ave. of the Americas, New York, NY 10019. The entire text has been published by Dramatists Play Service, 440 Park Ave. S., New York, NY 10016. 212-MU3-8960 (www.dramatists.com), who also handle performance rights.

Dog Sees God: Confessions of a Teenaged Blockhead. © 2006 by Bert V. Royal. Reprinted by permission of Chris Till, Paradigm, 500 5th Ave., 37th Fl., New York, NY 10110. The entire text has been published by Dramatists Play Service, 440 Park Ave. S., New York, NY 10016. 212-MU3-8960 (www.dramatists.com), who also handle performance rights.

Dues. © 2006 by Dwight C. Hobbes. All rights reserved. Reprinted by permission of Playscripts, Inc. To purchase acting editions of this play, which is part of the anthology *Point of Revue,* or to obtain stock or amateur performance rights, you must contact Playscripts, Inc. (Website: www.playscripts.com) (E-mail: info@playscripts.com). Phone: 866-NEW-PLAY (866-639-7529).

Indian Blood. © 2006 by A. R. Gurney. Reprinted by permission of Jonathan Lomma, William Morris Agency, Inc., 1325 Ave. of the Americas, New York, NY 10019. The entire text has been published by Broadway Play Publishing, Inc., 56 E. 81st St., New York, NY 10028-8358. 212-772-8334 (www.broadwayplaypubl.com), who also handle performance rights.

Leading Ladies. © 2006 by Ken Ludwig. Reprinted by permission of Jonathan Lomma, William Morris Agency, Inc., 1325 Ave. of the Americas, New York, NY 10019. The entire text has been published by Samuel French, Inc., 45 W. 25th St., New York, NY 10010. 212-206-8990. (www.samuelfrench.com), who also handle performance rights.

Levittown. © 2007 by Marc Palmieri. Reprinted by permission of the author. The entire text has been published by Dramatists Play Service, 440 Park Ave. S., New York, NY 10016. 212-MU3-8960 (www.dramatists.com), who also handle performance rights.

Life Science. © 2006 by Anna Ziegler. Reprinted by permission of Peregrine Whittlesey, 279 Central Park W. #23, New York, NY 10024. 212-787-1802 (pwwagy@aol.com), who also handles performance rights. Contact Peregrine Whittlesey for further information.

Manuscript. © 2006 by Paul Grellong. Reprinted by permission of Chris Till, Paradigm, 500 5th Ave., 37th Fl., New York, NY 10110. The entire text has been published by Dramatists Play Service, 440 Park Ave. S., New York, NY 10016. 212-MU3-8960 (www.dramatists.com), who also handle performance rights.

THE MISTAKES MADELINE MADE. © 2006 by Elizabeth Meriwether. Reprinted by permission of Val Day, William Morris Agency, 1325 Ave. of the Americas, New York, NY 10019. The entire text has been published by Dramatists Play Service, 440 Park Ave. S., New York, NY 10016. 212-MU3-8960 (www.dramatists.com), who also handle performance rights.

OVER THE TAVERN. © 2006 by Tom Dudzick. All rights reserved. Reprinted by permission of Playscripts, Inc. To purchase acting editions of this play, or to obtain stock or amateur performance rights, you must contact Playscripts, Inc. (Website: www.playscripts.com) (E-mail: info@playscripts.com). Phone: 866-NEW-PLAY (866-639-7529).

POOF!. © 2006 by Lynn Nottage. All rights reserved. Reprinted by permission of Playscripts, Inc. To purchase acting editions of this play, or to obtain stock or amateur performance rights, you must contact Playscripts, Inc. (Website: www.playscripts.com) (E-mail: info@playscripts.com). Phone: 866-NEW-PLAY (866-639-7529).

THE RADIANT ABYSS. © 2006 by Angus Maclachlan. Reprinted by permission of Peter Hagan, The Gersh Agency, 41 Madison Ave., New York, NY 10001. The entire text has been published by Dramatists Play Service, 440 Park Ave. S., New York, NY 10016. 212-MU3-8960 (www.dramatists.com), who also handle performance rights.

PUBLIC TRANSPORTATION. © 2006 by Warren C. Bowles. All rights reserved. Reprinted by permission of Playscripts, Inc. To purchase acting editions of this play, which is part of the anthology *Point of Revue*, or to obtain stock or amateur performance rights, you must contact Playscripts, Inc. (Website: www.playscripts.com) (E-mail: info@playscripts.com). Phone: 866-NEW-PLAY (866-639-7529).

SECRETARY OF SHAKE. © 2006 by Eisa Davis. All rights reserved. Reprinted by permission of Playscripts, Inc. To purchase acting editions of this play, which is part of the anthology *Point of Revue*, or to obtain stock or amateur performance rights, you must contact Playscripts, Inc. (Website: www.playscripts.com) (E-mail: info@playscripts.com). Phone: 866-NEW-PLAY (866-639-7529).

THE SPIRIT IS WILLING. © 2006 by Nicole Quinn. All rights reserved. Reprinted by permission of Playscripts, Inc. To purchase acting editions of this play, or to obtain stock or amateur performance rights, you must contact Playscripts, Inc. (Website: www.playscripts.com) (E-mail: info@playscripts.com). Phone: 866-NEW-PLAY (866-639-7529).

STRAIGHT ON TIL MORNING. © 2006 by Trish Harnetiaux. Reprinted by permission of the author. The entire text has been published by Broadway Play Publishing, Inc., 56 E. 81st St., New York, NY 10028-8358. 212-772-8334 (www.broadwayplaypubl.com), who also handle performance rights.